Elloraine Lothian is a suffering servant with resilience, character, stamina and unquenchable joy. She is real, her story is touching. Her life gives strong voice to the Christian theology of triumph in the midst of trials. Her story helps us to appreciate that prosperity goes beyond health and wealth. My Unexpected Journey is a must read.

Rev. Dr. Roy Notice,
President Bethel Bible College

In the pages of this book, you will meet one of God's special jewels – a real treasure of a young woman. Indeed she is a young woman of faith and courage – a young woman who has been tested through illness, yet has not succumbed to the suggestions of the enemy. Instead, she has remained steadfast and unmovable, secure in the knowledge that "God can be trusted to keep His promise" (Hebrews 10:23 – NLT).

It will bless you tremendously to meet this writer (even through her book), and understand that God still furnishes His children with sustaining grace.

Mrs. Evon Blair
Minister

Lessons Learned in the Valley of Pain

VOLUME ONE

ELLORAINE LOTHIAN

My Unexpected Journey

Copyright © 2010

ISBN #978-976-8217-95-2

Printed in Jamaica W.I. by Xpress Litho Ltd.

This book is dedicated to my father,
Mr. Emanuel Lothian.

Daddy, I just want you to know that any
determination and perseverance that flows through
my veins come from you. You have taught me
through your own life how to defy the odds, as time
and time again I have seen you rise triumphantly out
of the ashes of your life. Thank you for being my
greatest teacher.

Table of Contents

Foreword

Everyone is on a journey because life is a journey. For some the journey takes them across the sea, others, it is through the air, still for others it is on the land…Wherever it may be, the journey continues and sometimes takes some unexpected turns.

Such is Elloraine's journey. No one could have envisioned the winding curves, hilly terrain, deep precipices, dark valleys, insurmountable mountains and uncrossable rivers she would encounter; yet she, through her faith, has conquered.

Speaking of faith, I hasten to say her faith has taught me to *"hold to God's unchanging hand."* I believe with all my heart that this dear child of God is a rare gift to us, and as we go through this book, you will note it is going to be hard to put it down before completion. The chapters are self-explanatory, very simply written yet profound, and I admire how she approaches the different chapters, constantly reminding us that God alone deserves the glory.

I am challenged by her message to all of us. After sharing the Job-like experiences she goes beyond the "though God slay me" concept and sends a reminder to the devil: *"The difference between you and me is that I have a glorious hope beyond this life. When I leave this earth, my life begins for eternity; your future is destined for a bottomless pit forever. There is no hope for you; I will continue to remain steadfast."* Elloraine truly sends forth radiant beams through this book; she shares what she has learnt from her experience: *Only faith in God can sustain you through life's journey.* Read this book, digest it, and learn from her experience.

Bishop, The Rev. Dr. W. A. Blair

Acknowledgement

God, My Friend, My Lover, My Essence You gave me the command in July 2002 after my first major surgery to write a book. At first, I laughed thinking write a book? I am not a writer? It is now eight years later and I am ecstatic beyond words to say to you...here is that book. As your servant, I have humbly obeyed your command. I take no credit for this book. I was just a pen in your hand. To you be all the Glory and Honor.

To my editor, Miss Misha Lobban thank you for the many sacrifices of your devotion, and hours upon hours for making this book a reality. You are a treasure from heaven.

Thank you Mrs. Lois Gayle for all your invaluable suggestions and timely guidance, this book would not be complete without it. Thank you Carlalee Gowie, Nathalee Scott, and DaMariel for all the hours of proof reading, priceless suggestions, and your patience with me when I did not get it right. This project would not be finished without you.

My family has been a tower of strength to me during this difficult period of my life. I do not know how I would have survived without their love. They have consistently showered their passionate care and have carried me when I could not walk. Thank you.

To my parents, Mr. and Mrs. Emanuel Lothian, you have expressed your love and support for me in ways that I have never known prior to this experience. Words are unable to eloquently express my appreciation for all you have done.

Daddy, you have always supported me and I am honored to be called your daughter. God was smiling down on me when He gave me the awesome privilege of having you as my father. Love you from the depths of my heart.

Mrs. Lothian, (Auntie Claire) your compassion knows no bounds; I am eternally grateful for the love and care you have showered on me. I thank you, from the core of my heart, for supporting me on countless occasions during this challenging chapter of my life.

To my brothers (Carlie, Richie, Anthony, Newton, Lauren) I recall two visits by my brother, Carlie, while I was in the hospital. On one of those visits he said, *"Sis it rough inna di Gideon."* I placed my hand on my chest and we both laughed uncontrollably. When I was scheduled to do my fourth surgery he visited again and during that visit, he said, *"Sis it's not Gideon again it's 'Armagiddeon'."* Again, we laughed hysterically. Those moments were and are still priceless to me. Brother, the thought that has brought divine comfort to me is that Jesus is in my *'Gideon'* and *'Armagiddeon'* and that makes it alright.

To my sisters (Ava, Kayann, Sophia, Trecia, Shadeen); To my cousins (Verona, Mauvalyn, Lorna, Stephanie, Sherona, Geion, Sashana) to all my other relatives thank you. Thank you for the many visits while I was in the hospital. All the efforts you have made to make this experience bearable.

iv

To all my devoted friends the 'gang of six' (S.D.M.N.N.T.) you know who you are. To all the others I cannot write names because I would not have enough pages; Thank you guys ever so much. You all have a special place in my heart. I am humbled by your continued display of kindness and love…love you to pieces…

To my friend Cristo, I consider you my laughing partner for life. Thank you for the many moments of laughter. *"If I could reach up and hold a star for every time you've made me smile,* the entire evening sky would be in the palm of my hand."* [Anonymous]. Thank you for the gift of your presence, during this trying time.

To Bishop Dr. Ronald Blair and his wife Mrs. Evon Blair, you have been absolutely divine. Thank you so much for all you have done for me in this winter season of my life. I am forever grateful to you both. May God continue to overshadow you with His awesome presence and blessings perpetually.

To my church family at the Portmore New Testament Church of God; sisters and brothers in Christ, my prayer mothers, my prayer warriors; you have all been tremendous. I could not have made it this far without your faithful prayers, continued support and encouragement. Thank you, thank you from a heart of deep gratitude and love. May God eternally bless you.

To my pastor, Bishop Rev. Dr. W.A. Blair and his wife Mrs. Yvonne Blair. Your support has been amazing, words cannot express my gratitude. Thank you for your encouragement. Thank you for being my eternal cheerleaders. I could not have made it this far without your support. Blessings to you both everlastingly.

To my doctors, Dr. Roger Irvine, Dr. J. Blidgen, Dr. A. Coye, Dr. H. Shaw, Dr. S. Little, Dr. Jefferson, Dr. S.O.A.

Ononuju. Thanks for all the tender care you extended towards me, I am immensely grateful.

I have made careful efforts to locate copyright ownership of all material I quote in this book. If any readers of this book know the correct source(s) for items designated anonymous, I will appreciate hearing from you so corrections can be made and the appropriate credit given.

Elloraine Lothian:
This picture was taken during the writing of this book

Prologue

I was in the prime of my life when I was diagnosed with a rare form of tumor called Fibromatosis. Little did I know that four years later I would still be battling it. Life, as I had known it, would never be the same again. But throughout this challenging experience there was never a time when I wanted to give up on my relationship with my Lord. That, for me, was not an option. The Christian journey, in my view, is the greatest lifestyle that one could ever experience.

My initial reaction to the diagnosis was shock, disbelief and tears; lots of tears. But the thought that was of greatest comfort to me was, *"God makes no mistakes because He is a wise God. He knows exactly what is happening to me and I have to continue to trust Him even when I do not understand."*

For almost four years I have lived with constant pain. The first major surgery left me with a scar 17 inches long. I struggled to live a somewhat 'normal life' despite my circumstances. However, it was impossible for me to remain gainfully employed and consequently, meeting my financial obligations were challenging. But I have learned, and I am still learning, that God is truly my source so, I continue to trust Him. If I did not, there is no doubt in my mind that this ordeal would have driven me into a mental institution.

During my struggles I have often turned to the book of Job for strength, comfort and hope. It provided great insights for me as it revealed Job's attitude and emotions when his life was suddenly interrupted by several tragedies. It showed how his faith remained steadfast in spite of all his struggles. Personally, I believe that not only was Job's faith on trial but God's faith in him was also on trial. Like Job, my own faith had been challenged and as such I think Brother Job and I had several things in common. Here are some of the similarities that I have identified:

- Our faith was tested in the severest form.
- I went through most, if not all the emotions Job experienced - hopelessness, depression, sadness, weariness, anger, doubt.
- It seemed like God was silent and we became overwhelmed by unanswered questions concerning the trials we faced.
- At times we felt as if death was more appealing than life.

There was, however, one grave difference between Job and me – the kind of friends that he had. He called his friends 'miserable comforters.' My friends have all been my 'earth angels.' I am blessed with some of the most precious friendships in the world.

My experience has taught me that suffering has a way of refining our faith in God. To live a life of faith requires a good dose of perseverance. I know that God is able to sustain me through every difficult situation. Time and time again, I have mentioned in this book that as long as I cling to God I can handle anything life throws my way.

A new and deeper intimacy and love for God has also blossomed from the seed of suffering planted by this tumor. I am now at a place where I have surrendered the outcome of my illness to God. Whether I live or die there is nothing more important than my relationship and faith in Him.

During my journey with this illness, I have realized that life comes with different processes and so I have to survive with each moment. I went through an emotional purgatory that has left me resolute in saying that giving up is not an option. God's strength and grace have taught me to be content in spite of my situation. I know that I will come out of this experience with a fortitude that defies description and with what I call *Loyalty Faith*. Faith that is immune to the notion of giving up.

The many lessons and the wisdom that I have gained from my experiences are included in a summary at the end of each chapter - Reflections on Life's Lessons. I can honestly say that my faith has matured immeasurably. Yes, I have indeed found purpose in suffering.

As you read this book, I hope that it will strengthen your own faith in God and be a source of encouragement as you go through difficult times in your life. May it inspire you to continue to believe that there is purpose in your valley experiences and that at the end of it all you will see that God was working things out for your good.

As I invite you to share in this story which is coming from my heart, I would like you to know that my expressions of confidence in God and my determination to keep true to Him are based solely on His grace towards me and not on anything of credit on my part. Like the Apostle Paul I have nothing in which to glory apart from the Cross of Jesus Christ my Lord - Galatians 6:14 -KJV.

<u>Please note</u>
The events of this book
span the period October
2001- December 2005.
This text was prepared
in the year 2006,
as a result throughout this
book you will see that
I consistently say I have been
going through this illness
for the past four years.
That is, I was diagnosed
in the year 2002 but in 2006
I was still battling the tumor.
Note that no events of 2006
are recorded on these pages.
I believe that, God willing,
there will definitely be
another book to complete
this season of my life...
*stay glued as the journey
continues to unfold.*

My
Unexpected
Journey

Mild What???

I n my mind I was in the prime of my life. I was 26 years old and a few years prior, had completed my first degree, a Bachelor's in accounting and management. At this point, I was making preparations to do my second degree. I had it all planned out. I would be married by the time I was 28, I would have three children. Life was going to be good. I felt youthful and strong. I had a zest for life and the perseverance that would pave my way to success. I had determination and tenacity of purpose.

I started experiencing pain in my left hand between October and December 2001. At first, I didn't think much of it because it was irregular but I vividly remember that on December 21, 2001, the pain in my hand lasted for the entire night. This had never happened

3

before and it ached all over. The Christmas season came and went but the pain continued. By this time, it had become constant and had extended to my neck and upper back. I thought it would eventually go away but when it didn't I realized something was seriously wrong. I then decided to visit my general practitioner, Dr. Themba Deane.

The results coming out of that visit were that my blood pressure was too high, I may have suffered a mild stroke and there was a "murmur" on my heart. I sat there thinking, *"Who is he talking about? Mild stroke and the name Elloraine are not spoken in the same sentence...You have got to be kidding!!!"* Kidding he was not. It was really obvious that something was wrong with me. Dr. Deane instructed me to have some tests done. These included X–rays, an electrocardiogram (ECG) and blood tests.

An ECG is done to record the electrical rhythms of the heart within a given time frame to see if there are any irregularities. My ECG test result showed that my heartbeat was normal. The X-rays showed that there was a large mass of tissue on the left side of my neck extending into my thoracic cavity (chest area).

No definite conclusions could have been drawn from these preliminary tests, so I was instructed to do a Computed Tomography Scan (CT scan) of the neck and chest area as it was a more detailed test than the X-ray. As the days passed, I felt like someone else was living inside my body. This could not be happening to me. But indeed *it was* happening to me.

The result of the CT scan was definitely not good. It confirmed what was seen on the X-ray. There was a large mass at the left side of my neck extending into the upper chest area. It was about the size of a large grapefruit. It was compressing a major and important vein that ran from my brain through the neck and into my chest. As a result, many other veins had developed to overcome the obstruction. The mass was eroding one of the vertebrae called T1 and it was pushing my esophagus out of its rightful position. The result of the scan concluded that this was a nerve tumor. At that time, no one knew whether or not it was cancerous.

My initial reaction to these findings was shock, disbelief and tears, lots of tears. When I tried to inform family members about the results of the CT scan my mouth could not properly form the words. Tears, coupled with gasping breaths between sobs made it difficult for me to speak. After some time had passed, I sobered up and the tears subsided. Somehow a sense of calm, like a deep, still ocean of peace enveloped me. It was as if the tears had temporarily washed away the bad news.

I was scheduled to see Dr. Deane the following Sunday (February 17, 2002) so I had a few days to process all that was happening. During those days I reflected on the events of the previous months.

Between the months of December 2001 and February 2002, I had sensed in my spirit that something was imminent. I didn't understand it, but it was as if my spirit was preparing me for all that was about to take place. During one particular Youth Service at my church, my worship experience was different. I remember crying so hard that I literally could not stand on my own; someone had to support me.

I sensed that I was crying in the present for a future tragedy. I also recalled attending a Choir Retreat in February 2002, where I made a new covenant with God. I told Him that my own will no longer mattered; I was totally surrendered to His will. *"If you can use anything use me. I want to be more than an ordinary servant."* On reflection, I would have retracted that prayer because never in a million years did I think I would be going through this long and painful process. But I believe that God was preparing me for all that I was going to experience. It was evident that I was in a different phase of my Christian life, and new spiritual experiences had begun.

I was amazingly calm when I visited Dr. Deane. He commented on how calm I was yet he had this worried look on his face. I thought to myself, *"The doctor looks worried about the results; this cannot be good!"* After that meeting, I was introduced to a new team. They assessed the various tests that I had previously done and later informed me that I had *"Plexiform Neurofibroma"* (a complex term for *nerve tumor*).

Neurofibromas are tumors which come from the sheath around the nerves. They are generally benign. They are made of cells that form the nerve sheath, for example, fibroblasts (cells that make up scar tissue) as well as schwaan cells (cells that line the nerves). Plexiform Neurofibromas are Neurofibromas that spread out, just under the skin or deeper inside the body. The word "plexus" refers to a combination of interlaced parts or a network. This type of Neurofibroma can grow in many different places, such as on the face, the leg or the spinal column and can cause severe disfiguration.

As I tried to comprehend the diagnosis, the doctors confessed that my case was unique, mainly because it was located in a complicated and delicate area. The tumor stemmed from the nerve of the vertebrae and extended into the upper chest area. After this initial diagnosis, I was told that I needed to do a biopsy. This was to facilitate further investigation so that more appropriate decisions could be made regarding treatment and the best

6

possible way to remove the mass of tissue without causing major harm.

On March 1, 2002, I was admitted to the hospital to do a biopsy. It was my first hospital experience since I was seven years old. While there, many questions began to assault my mind: *Why was I here? Yes, to do a biopsy but what is the spiritual significance? Who will I meet and how can I touch their lives?* I asked God to help me to clearly see His purpose in all of this. I asked Him to keep my spiritual antennae tuned, so that I would not miss any valuable lessons that I should learn from this experience.

One of the many things that I have learned throughout this whole journey is that at times a person's presence is all that matters. Sometimes all you need to do is to show up for someone in their time of need. In the movie, "Hard Ball" Conor O'Neill, played by Keanu Reeves summed it up perfectly when he said to his team, *"...One of the most important things in life is showing up. I'm blown away by your ability to show up..."*

On Sunday, March 03, 2002, 26 persons including family members, friends and well wishers came to visit me. An avalanche of grateful emotions swept over me. I thought to myself all these people came to see me... all 26 of them! I was ecstatic, overjoyed, overwhelmed, and moved beyond tears. So, it was only natural that I was grinning from ear to ear with my 'camera-ready smile.' At that point, although my body was still in pain I was too busy reveling in the presence of my visitors to feel it. I thought, *"Life is good. God is good. I will come out of this soon."*

Later that evening, the pain intensified and lasted throughout the night. With tears in my eyes, all I kept thinking was, *"Pain, go ahead and attack me with all your might but you cannot erase the fact that 26 persons came to see me today and that's because I'm loved...I am special."* That's what got me through the night.

Since the age of 15, I have been journaling. So it was typical that I had my journal with me. This is one of my entries during my stay at the hospital.

March 03, 2002

Sometimes God, I feel like I am part of something that is big. I cannot imagine what it is. I just sense that this is going to be something that is huge; bigger than I can imagine but I have all the confidence that You will be with me.

Through it all I have learnt to trust in You. I've learnt to find comfort in Your Word.

March 06, 2002, was the day of the biopsy. Many thoughts were flooding my mind. I was nervous and a bit fearful and the fact that I was the first person on the list for surgery did not make it any easier. Everything seemed a bit unreal. I kept asking myself, *"Is this really happening?"*

Whether I thought it was, or not, at that exact moment I was wheeled towards the operating theatre and parked outside the entrance. I smiled at the image of me being parked like a car. I used the phrase 'parked' because the porter took so much care to align my gurney perfectly at the door. He did it with such precision as one would if he or she were doing a driving test.

Once again, I was alone with my thoughts. I said to myself, *"Am I really going into the operating theatre?"* Well, that question was answered shortly after, as I was taken into the theatre with its huge lights, machines and other complex-looking equipment. I had requested that the intravenous infusion (IV) be placed in my right hand to avoid any additional pain in my left hand. I felt relieved to see that this small request was honored. My feet were strapped to the table and the last thing I remember was the oxygen mask being placed over my face. Then I was out like a light.

I was told the procedure lasted for approximately three hours. I was in and out of consciousness when I realized that I was being prepared to do an X-ray. For the remainder of the day I felt extremely helpless. I must have looked terrible because I could feel this huge bandage on my neck where a small incision was made. My chest felt extremely painful and uncomfortable. It felt as if a bulldozer had been parked on it. My eyes were very teary because of the ordeal.

Sometime later, I was told that I had a visitor. It was Sophia. I was blown away. Why? We were not close friends as yet. I was stunned to see that she came to visit me and I burst into tears. I wasn't crying because of the pain and discomfort but because of an overwhelming feeling of gratitude and appreciation for the visit. Through my tears I thanked her for coming to see me.

As the day progressed, I drifted in and out of sleep. It was painful to move, cough, swallow, smile, belch, yawn, sigh or do just about anything. I was thirsty and hungry but to attempt to eat anything felt like a death sentence. Intense pain racked my body. My stepmother (I affectionately call her Auntie Claire), daddy, my brother Carlie, a family friend (Miss Darling) and my best friend

Nathalee arrived later that day. By this time, tears fell effortlessly from my eyes. Daddy and Carlie could not bear to see me cry, so they went outside for a while. My visitors appeared as if they were baptized in sadness. So, to break the ice, I told Nathalee, who was assisting me to drink a cup of tea, that she was doing it with careful precision as if she were feeding her two-year-old nephew. For a short time laughter erupted in the room. Auntie Claire sensed how helpless I was and so she tried to make me as comfortable as possible.

I had made it a priority not to look sick during my stay in the hospital. I remember a popular preacher saying, *"You might be going through the fire but you don't have to smell like smoke."* That statement had become a major gem in my life. But with all my effort after the surgery, I know I looked sick and helpless.

The day after the surgery was much better but I still felt as if a bulldozer was on my chest, only this time it was moving. Except for the bandages and a noticeably swollen neck I thought I looked pretty good, therefore, I was hoping that I would be sent home.

During the course of the day I was sent to do an X-ray and to my disappointment I was told that I had to stay overnight for observation.

Hallelujah!!! Friday came and I was packed and ready to go home. I was the happiest person alive. One of the main reasons I was ecstatic about going home was the fact that my birthday was only three days away and I did not want to spend it in the hospital.

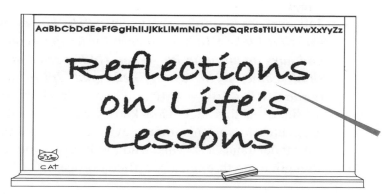

AaBbCcDdEeFfGgHhIiJjKkLlMmNnOoPpQqRrSsTtUuVvWwXxYyZz

Reflections on Life's Lessons

- Visit persons you know who are in the hospital. Do not be concerned that you do not have anything to give. That pales in comparison to the importance of your presence. It could be the reason that the person made it through the night. Sometimes your presence is all that is needed. Your job is to just show up. That's how you can help in the healing process.

- As a child of God, it is not always easy to understand the challenging experiences that He allows us to endure. Sometimes He will lead where you never thought or imagined you would go; sometimes it may cost you more than you are willing to pay. However, I had one consoling thought after hearing that initial diagnosis: It was that, *"God is not surprised by what is happening for He knows the end from the beginning."* So I know He was not in heaven with hands akimbo saying to Jesus; *"Did you hear what happened to Elloraine?"* Words like Isaiah's **"Declaring the end from the beginning..."** (46:10 - KJV) comforted me; God knew how this would finish before it ever started.

11

- **Job** expressed similar sentiments: *"He knows the way that I take [He has concern for it, appreciates, and pays attention to it]. When He has tried me, I shall come forth as refined gold [pure and luminous]"* (23:10 - AMP). Grab a hold of and meditate on this fact: God knows exactly what is happening to you this minute even though you may not understand it. This truth will give you the strength to go through any difficult process.

- Don't lean on your own understanding, if you do, you may be tempted to walk away from your relationship with God because the circumstances do not add up. Secretly you may ask yourself, *"How could God allow this to happen?"* In my own situation, I knew in my spirit that God was with me, and one of my reassuring Scriptures was, *"Lean on, trust in, and be confident in the Lord with all your heart and mind and do not rely on your own insight or understanding. In all your ways know, recognize, and acknowledge Him and He will direct and make straight and plain your paths."* (Proverb 3:5 – 6 - AMP).

Worst Case Scenario

It was real
It was happening to me
I denied it
I tried to push it out of my mind
The inconceivable had happened!
It was happening to me!

Maybe if I pretend it would go away
But I'm still here and illness clings to me
Worst case scenario
No
This was real.

So what do I do now?
What do you do when life as you know it
ceases to exist?
When the patterns and paths you've carved
Become shadowed, darkened, and destroyed?
What do I do?

Alone, there's little comfort
I don't want to do this alone but that's how I feel
I scrape for courage at the bottom of my soul
Just to show a brave face
But the weight of my tragedy causes courage
to scamper away

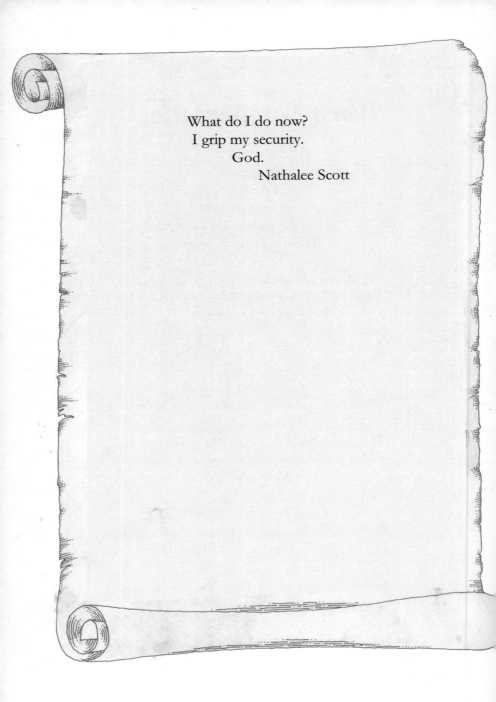

What do I do now?
I grip my security.
God.
Nathalee Scott

My
Unexpected
Journey

Tears, Tears, Tears and more Tears

Even though I had been in constant pain since the beginning of 2002, after the March 6 biopsy it seemed as if my body went haywire. Constant pain, coupled with lack of sleep, was the order of the day. I was miserable and I cried a lot because of the intensity of the pain. During these times Auntie Claire proved to be a compassionate companion. She was my talking and crying partner for several hours during the night.

There are indeed times when all you can do to help a relative or friend is to just cry with them. It may not seem like much but it speaks volumes. That is love in action.

The first sign of sleep came on Saturday night when my father slept by my side. I was tossing and turning and then the thought popped into my mind, *"Why not use daddy's stomach as a pillow?"* I rested my head on his stomach and then came my first four hours of undisturbed sleep since I left the hospital. I was so grateful that daddy had a large tummy to accommodate me. I no longer thought it was too big; it was now the perfect size. With God's help I managed to survive that weekend.

Monday, March 11 came; it was my birthday! It was the most memorable birthday I had to date. Family and friends came to celebrate with me. Even though I was tired from lack of sleep, it was not obvious. I enjoyed having them around me. I smiled and took pictures…lots of pictures. The real pain came when everyone left. Only God knew how I survived. It was as if the pain just waited for everyone to leave and then it started to attack. But in my mind I declared, *'Pain go ahead, just remember I know I'm loved and appreciated by my family and friends and at this point that is all that matters.'*

The result of the biopsy confirmed the diagnosis that I had Plexiform Neurofibroma. It was deemed a complicated case. The good news was that this type of tumor was non-cancerous. Thank God!!! I was instructed to do an even more detailed form of X-ray called a Magnetic Resonance Imaging (MRI). This was in an effort to identify the exact position of the tumor, the veins that ran through it and to gain additional information on how the surgeons could proceed in attempting to remove it. The MRI scan proved to be sheer torture because I had to lie on my back for approximately 25 minutes. This made the pain I was experiencing even more unbearable.

Sometime after the MRI scan was done, I had a meeting with the head surgeon for the cardiothoracic team, Dr. Roger Irvine. At that meeting, it was decided that surgery would be scheduled for May 2, 2002 and the remaining days in the month of April were basically preparation for the surgery. I told him to give me some time to prepare myself physically, including doing my hair (sorry, I was just being a typical woman). You wouldn't believe that I was feeling intense pain yet I was concerned about trivial things like a hair-do, but I was determined to look my best because I knew that after a surgery of that magnitude for the next two months I would not be able to properly take care of myself or my appearance.

By all indications (at least in my mind) I shouldn't be sick. During one of the many conversations with my brother Carlie, he asked, *"Chris (my pet name) how is it that you are sick? Compared to all of us you eat the healthiest and you are disciplined with your exercises. You shouldn't be sick."* I smiled because in my heart I was thinking the very same thing.

On Monday, April 22, daddy and I met with Dr. Irvine to get feedback on the result of the MRI scan and details about the surgery that I would do on May 2.

The result of the MRI Scan of the neck and chest showed that there was a large mass lying beside the vertebrae (back bone) in the lower neck and extending into the chest. The mass caused some destruction to three of the vertebrae that run from the lower neck to the

19

upper chest where it lies adjacent to them. The mass also encroached on the part of the vertebrae where important nerves and blood vessels leave and enter the spinal cord. It also encased one of the arteries supplying the brain, the nerves and blood vessels that leave and enter the spinal cord in the upper chest.

The mass indented the top of the left lung and was adjacent to the arch of the aorta and the blood vessels above the heart.

Dr. Irvine further explained that one of the arteries that carries blood to my brain was entangled with the tumor and as a result it was not functioning as it should. It was quite likely that I would eventually lose the function of this artery. To say that I was overwhelmed by all this information would be a grave understatement. As he continued to speak, I began to lose my composure and tears started to stream down my face. I was floored when he told me about the size of the incision that would be required to remove the tumor. The sobs that I had so desperately tried to subdue freely erupted. I recall Dr. Irvine saying that he worried about me all weekend and I thought to myself, *"If you are the surgeon and you are worried, can you imagine what the patient is going through?"* I appreciated Dr. Irvine so much because he was so compassionate. He wasn't afraid to let me know his fears and concerns. I remember looking into his eyes while I cried and I may be mistaken but I thought I saw traces of tears in them. In my mind I shouted, *"Thank you for being considerate, thank you for the tears, thank you for being real!"*

On my way home from the meeting, the tears really fell in a downpour. I cried for many reasons but mainly because I had begun to mourn the death of my chest; I was bewailing a part of me that would never be the same after surgery. This must have been how Jephthah's daughter felt when she asked for time to bewail her virginity, or as some versions of the Bible explained, she bewailed the fact that she would never experience the joy of marriage.

The story is told in **Judges 11:29 – 40.** Jephthah, the commander of the Gileadite army, was about to go to war against the Ammonities but before doing so he made a vow to the Lord, saying,. *"...If you give the Ammonities into my hands, whatever comes out of the door of my house to meet me when I return in triumph from the Ammonities will be the Lord's and I will sacrifice it as a burnt offering"* (30-31-NIV)

Jephthath defeated the Ammonities. The first person to greet him when he returned home after the war was his daughter - his only child. Jephthah was distraught but he had to keep his promise to the Lord and his daughter encouraged him in this. But she had one request before being offered up as a sacrifice: *"...Give me two months to roam the hills and weep with my friends, because I will never marry"* (37-NIV). In essence, she was saying *'Give me the time to mourn, give me the time to accept the consequence of your vow to the Lord. After I have mourned and accepted my reality then I will return and do as you vowed to the Lord.'* She mourned for two months with her friends and then returned to her father prepared to face the inevitable.

Unlike Jephthah's daughter I did not have the luxury of two months to mourn. My period of mourning was approximately one week and I did it without friends. It began on my way home from the meeting with Dr. Irvine on April 22. I had to accept my reality. So, I held my chest for a very long time and cried my eyes out. That's the last time I remember crying for my chest. Later I wrote in my journal:

Journal Entry: April 22, 2002

I wailed for some time because everything was so overwhelming. I was numb with disbelief. I could not speak because I really did not know what to say. I was at a loss for words. One could see the fear and sorrow in my father's eyes as he thought I had crumbled to pieces. However, I don't want him to confuse my being emotional with hopelessness... they are two different things...

This process that I am going through calls for a sacrifice of my body; it is costing me my once normal body (at least, I thought it was normal). I decided, *"God, it is okay with me as long as it is okay with you. I gave you my life 11 years ago and now I have to believe that you have my best interest at heart, no matter how bad it seems."* I told God again I trusted Him and that I knew He was not surprised by all that was happening to me. Like the Scripture states, ***"...Do not be surprised at the painful trial you are*** *suffering, as though something strange were happening to you"* (1 Peter 4:12 -NIV).

During the days leading up to the surgery I prayed and asked God to give me an unshakeable peace; I prayed for the peace that Paul invoked for the **Philippian** brethren: *"And God's peace [shall be yours, that tranquil state of a soul assured of its salvation through Christ, and so fearing nothing from God and being content with its earthly lot of whatever sort that is, that peace] which transcends all understanding shall garrison and mount guard over your hearts and minds in Christ Jesus"* (4:7-AMP).

Faithfully, God answered in two ways. Firstly, out of nowhere, the Holy Spirit brought to the forefront of my mind the song, "Trust His Heart" by Babbie Mason. This song had been a significant part of my life in the 90s when I was a young Christian. It became a source of comfort during the days leading up to the surgery. Here is an excerpt:

*"God is too wise to be mistaken…
So when you don't understand…
When you can't trace His hand
Trust His heart."*

I clung to the thought that God makes no mistakes. Irrespective of the constant pain, the sleepless nights and the seriousness of the surgery, God has promised never to leave me nor forsake me and that was an irrefutable fact.

Secondly, I received a call from Markel, one of my friends. As we conversed he said, *"Elloraine, when we say 'Lord I'm available to You' it's not just our service, it also means our bodies and if need be our lives. Our heart's cry should be 'Lord, my body is available to You, use it for Your will."* Right at that moment I understood the magnitude of my commitment 11 years ago. I had been on the youth choir for many years and had sung the song, "I'm Available to You" written by Carlis Moody Junior, countless times. Here is an excerpt:

"Lord I'm available to You
My will I give to You
I'll do what you say…"

This song was my declaration vow to God. *"Now how could I go back on my word? Elloraine, why are you now not practising what you have been singing? Didn't you mean it?"* I asked myself. It was then I realized that we need to be careful of the words we utter unto God because He will hold us accountable for them. I knew I was about to take the biggest test of my Christian life and failure was not an option. I now understood that my faithful church attendance; reading and studying God's Word and listening to many inspiring sermons were only preparation for this big moment.

I was admitted to the hospital on April 30, to begin routine preparation for the surgery on May 2. In the natural, I was a young woman about to do major surgery but spiritually, I was a pit bull dog ready for a challenge. Without fear, I faced the devil with a resolve that said, *"I'm not afraid. Take your best shot. Try all you want but I'm coming at you with the peace of God and I have no intention of backing down. Whatever happens beyond this point does not matter. In life or death, I'm still a winner."* I was going along with Paul: ***"For to me to live is***

Christ, and to die is gain" **(Philippians 1:21 - KJV).** I was sealed with God's peace and I knew at this point that I was solely surviving with the help of the Holy Spirit.

May 1, the day before the surgery, was very busy. An interesting bit of news came to light. I knew they were contemplating placing cervical plates in my neck because the tests revealed that two of my vertebrae had been badly eroded. What I didn't know was that they were planning to remove both vertebrae and replace them with the plates. I thought to myself, *"I must have misunderstood; this is the day before the surgery, why didn't anyone tell me this? I thought they would be supporting the vertebrae not removing them all together!!!"* I had placed this surgery into God's hand and that was the end of the matter. Whatever happened I was prepared for the outcome.

After discussions with the neurosurgeon, it was decided to leave my vertebrae untouched. On the inside I was smiling from ear to ear satisfied that this proposal was cancelled.

I must admit that any rational person who saw me on the day before the surgery would have been stunned. I was busy talking with my doctors; looking at the MRI films to understand what was happening and having them address my concerns. I just kept my focus, having ongoing internal dialogues. Finally, all I could do was believe and trust God. This was no multiple choice examination, there was no a, b, c, d, or e option. There was only one answer - trust. Fear, doubt, worry and anxiety were negative emotions I could not afford to entertain.

"Worry drives a dagger of slander under the fifth rib of God's character." [Anonymous] This is a famous phrase of my pastor Bishop, the Rev. Dr. W. A. Blair. I did not fully understand the mystery of this saying; but the little I perceived was that worry destroys God's character. I did not want to do that. Instead, I clung to the Holy Spirit for supernatural strength.

In the evening, during visiting hours, my family, including Carlie, Mauvalyn and Auntie Claire as well as my friends Melissa, Jason, Vanessa, Claudette and Simone came to see me. I received two pounds of grapes from Jason and Vanessa and I ate every last one of them. My relatives were amazed at how calmly I sat eating the grapes. I remember saying to them, *"I'm not going to let them go to waste I have to stop eating by 10:00 o' clock tonight, so I'm on a roll here."*

Thursday, May 2, was finally here. I was up by 6:00 a.m., showered and ready for the surgery. Inside the operating theatre, I met the medical team. I recognized most of them from previous meetings. There were two sets of surgeons. One from the Ear Nose and Throat (ENT) team to remove the portion of the tumor from the neck and the other from the cardiothoracic team would remove the portion from the chest. I returned their greetings with my *'camera-ready smile.'* On the subject of the camera, I had asked one of the medical students to take as many pictures as he could of the procedure. I know you may be wondering, 'why pictures?' One, I am a fanatic of photos and two; I just wanted to see how my body looked on the inside. I had this body for 27 years and I thought the surgeons should not be the only ones having the privilege of seeing my insides. I wanted to see it too!!!

I fell asleep some time after 8:00 o'clock on Thursday morning and awoke in the recovery room at some time on Friday morning. The surgery itself, and preparation for it, lasted approximately eight hours. Tubes and IVs were inserted into my body but spiritually I was at peace. They said I did so well that I was not admitted to the Intensive Care Unit. Thank God!!!

As far as I was concerned it was all God. I really have no recollection of what occurred on Friday but on Saturday I felt like an invalid; helpless, weak and experiencing great discomfort. I had a tube in my neck and one in my side attached to a gallon sized bottle that I had to move around with; this alone was sheer torture. I had an IV in my hand and occasionally I had to wear an oxygen mask.

Sunday was a much better day. I was able to walk around briefly, and the oxygen mask was removed. The IV in my hand and the tube in my neck were also removed. I remember my first telephone conversation with my father. I was ecstatic to hear that he was on the line and without thinking, the first words out of my mouth were, *"Daddy, how are you doing?"* I remember him saying, *"Chris, I'm the one who should be asking you that." "I'm* fine Daddy." I answered. I wanted him to hear my voice and know that I was okay. My father was really worried about me. He thought I didn't understand the magnitude of everything but the truth is I understood all too well. I just knew that I was going to get passed this.

By Monday, May 6, I felt like my body was back to normal. On Tuesday, I was beaming from ear to ear and doing cartwheels in my mind because of the many visitors I received. I felt so blessed in spite of the large bandage extending from the left side of my neck down to my abdomen. That night I cried uncontrollably. *Why did I cry?* I cried because I was grateful and happy to be alive. God had been so good to me. When I saw the outpouring of love from my relatives, friends and church family, I was enveloped in a blanket of gratitude and emotions; I felt really loved.

I was released on Wednesday May 8, six days after the surgery. I could not believe it!!! I never thought that I would be released so soon but this surgery had God's signature affixed to it.

Yes, the surgeons did a great job but the 'Leading Surgeon' – God, My Father, did an even greater job! No wonder the Apostle Paul was moved to exalt our God and King with the words:

> *"Now to Him Who, by (in consequence of) the [action of His] power that is at work within us, is able to [carry out His purpose and] do superabundantly, far over and above all that we [dare] ask or think [infinitely beyond our highest prayers, desires, thoughts, hopes, or dreams]"* (Ephesians 3: 20 - AMP).

After the surgery, I had a new appreciation for the little things in life. I have learned to appreciate a sigh, a cough, a sneeze and a deep breath. When your breast bone is broken believe me the last thing you want to do is to sigh. Taking a deep breath was precious. We all have to remember to be appreciative of the little things in life. Now I know how fortunate I was before surgery.

My Bishop came to visit me on May 12; this was a defining moment for me. He told me he was impressed with my faith. *"Faith? What faith?! Is that what it is?"* I pondered on his words. *"You are an excellent teacher,"* I uttered inaudibly. *"I am just a student in your faith university."* Until this conversation I never perceived the depth of my faith; my only concern was not to disappoint God. At the end of the visit my conclusion was, *"My faith is on trial, but for how long?"*... I had no idea.

Rev. Dr. W.A. Blair and I at my birthday party,
March, 2002.

"Daddy and I smiling away at the birthday party

Daddy, Myself & Auntie Claire

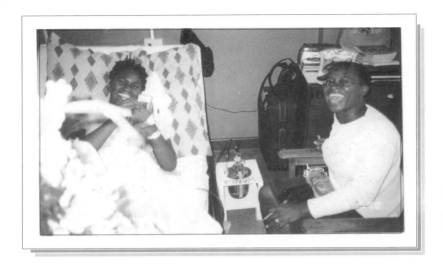

Simone and I cracking up at some joke

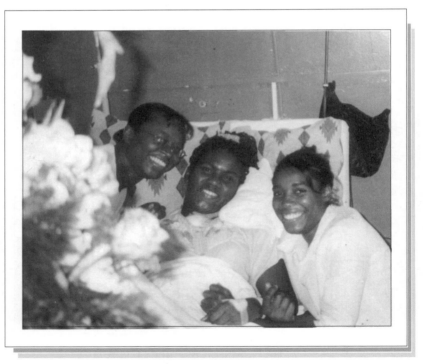

Simone, myself & Nathalee

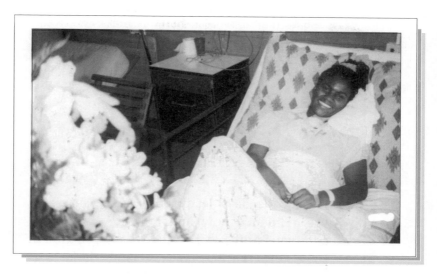

"Chilaxing" on a hospital bed

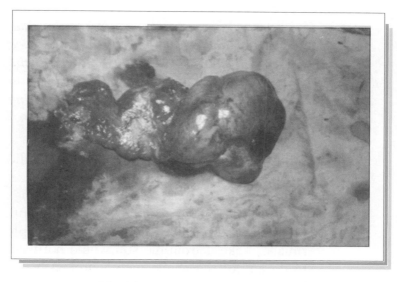

The biggest portion of the tumor
removed during surgery May 2002

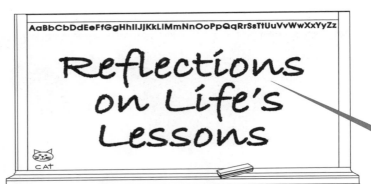

- During the days leading up to the surgery I was reminded how important it was to be conscious of the words that we utter to God in song or prayer. Why? God holds us accountable for them. The truth is, God may decide to test you and prove if your words are sincere. Hear the words of the wise man, Solomon, on the matter:

  > *"So when you make a promise to God, don't delay in following through, for God takes no pleasure in fools. Keep all the promises you make to him. It is better to say nothing than to promise something that you don't follow through on."* (Ecclesiastes 5: 4 – 5 –NLT)

- Before my breast bone was broken I really did not realize what a privilege it was to sneeze, sigh, cough or to take a deep breath…things we take for granted. Always remember how blessed you are to be able to do these simple rituals. Take it from me you would not want to do any of the above with a broken breast bone.

34

Will I Be Whole Again???

I look in the mirror and I don't recognize me.
A closer yet deeper look but still no clue:
A sigh escapes my lips as I wonder what to do

My body seems foreign.
Areas once alive, now dead to my touch
I can't believe this has happened to me
"Oh Lord I cried in dismay
Will I be whole again?!

Beauty has eluded me;
I don't believe when they say that
"the scar is no big deal".
They don't see the questioning looks
when I go for a meal.
Crushed, bruised, lost
When will I be whole again?
He promised me that my chest would be alright
But at times it seems like that's not in sight

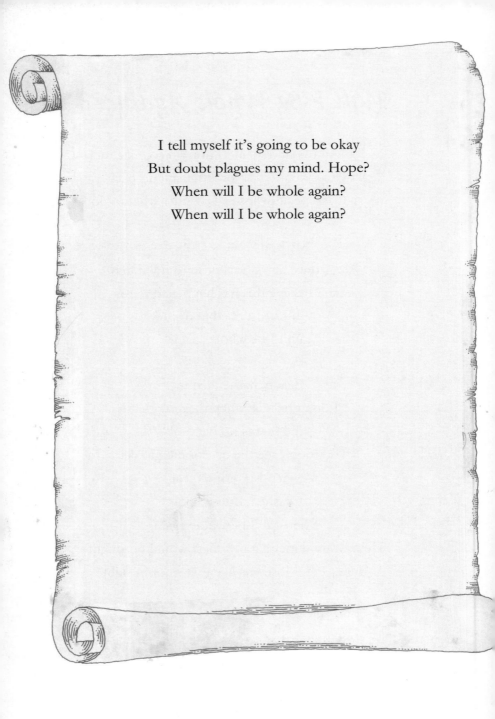

I tell myself it's going to be okay
But doubt plagues my mind. Hope?
When will I be whole again?
When will I be whole again?

My
Unexpected
Journey

The Tumor is Back!!!

For the first time in almost six months I was pain free and felt somewhat 'normal' again. No more pain killers. These were happy, happy, happy days. After the surgery on May 2, 2002, the doctors told me that they were able to remove about 95% of the tumor. The remaining portion was not visible to the naked eye.

A small drawback to the surgery was that I developed a slight ptosis in my left eye (that is my left eye lid is a bit lower than the right eye lid giving the appearance that my left eye is smaller than the right). This occurred because they had to sever some of my sympathetic nerves during the surgery as the tumor was entangled within them. As a result, I no longer sweat on the left side of my face. It's actually quite fascinating to see the right side of my face glistening while the other side is the opposite.

39

I also had to get used to the scar resulting from the surgery. I recalled gazing into the mirror and saying, *"God, this scar is really huge but I trust you and believe that all of this is according to your divine plan for my life."* Curious to know its length, I decided to measure it; it was 17 inches long!!! I have received countless stares and comments because of this scar. At times, I had to ask persons not to stare, and instead encouraged them to ask me about it. I had no problem telling persons about my situation but I couldn't deal with the stares. However, after a time, it really did not matter anymore.

I have learned that I had to find a 'new normal.' As we travel on this journey called 'life,' we go through situations that sometimes change our lives dramatically. For example, a person experiences a motor vehicle accident and ends up in a wheelchair; life is not what it used to be but you learn a 'new normal' and go on living. So, in my case I have learned to go about my daily life immune to people's stares.

In the months following the surgery, I had to do many follow-up visits for new developments. During those times I learned new lessons on the subject of patience. On one particular visit to the clinic, I waited six hours before being treated, and so to avoid getting frustrated I read different magazines and books. When I got bored, I started to write poems. During one of those very long waiting periods, I wrote the poem "Answers," (see page 51). I later revised it with the help of my friend, Earle Stewart.

In early August, I started to once again experience the pain I had felt between October and December of 2001. I did not understand why the pain had returned. I was getting used to the idea that my body would be pain free and back to normal. So I pondered: *"The tumor was removed so, what is causing this renewed pain?"*

I became really concerned, so I decided to inform Dr. Irvine. When I did, he promptly told me to come in for a visit and to do an X-ray.

The result of the X-ray is included in the following journal entry.

Journal Entry: August 7, 2002

On Tuesday, August 6, 2002 I went to do an X-ray. The result was not good. Dr. Irvine explained that the tumor was growing back again based on what he saw on the X-ray. Of course, I cannot believe what he said. As a matter of fact, I do not accept it. I was told this tumor is slow-growing and after three months you are telling me that it's now growing back!!! God, I cannot believe that I only had three months of living a normal life without pain. By the way, Dr. Irvine even mentioned that another surgery was necessary. Of course, I am thinking he must be crazy!!! Right there and then I told him nobody is going back inside my body. I cannot mentally undergo another surgery. Do you understand the magnitude of what you are telling me to accept? Dr. Irvine, are you crazy? God, how can allow this to happen? I cannot do another surgery. I just can't...

During the weeks following that visit to Dr. Irvine, the constant pain that I had known so well returned. Some days I cried. Some days I sighed. Some days I was simply numb. I thought to myself, *"There is no way I'm going to do another surgery. In fact, God, it is okay if you give me eternal sleep now, because what Dr. Irvine is suggesting is too much for my fragile mind to comprehend or to accept."*

I became militant against the devil. I claimed my healing and believed the Lord to do something miraculous for me. When I could not endure the pain any longer pain killers became my best friends. Although they never took the pain away completely, they lowered its intensity and that made life more tolerable. I started to seek God's counsel and direction. He had led me this far and I did not believe that He would leave me now.

I recalled looking at the photos of the May 2002 surgery; I looked like a slaughtered animal. Indeed, I felt like I was being sacrificed. The photos were not the easiest things to look at but I did not regret having them taken. They caused me to have a renewed sense of awe for God and then I realized that they could be a good witnessing tool for persons going through a challenging season in their lives. I can say to that individual, *"This was me, yet God was with me. Whatever you are going through, God will help you as He did me. Somehow this all fits into His plan for our lives. Our duty is to just trust Him."*

God does everything strategically and in His time and it always works out for His purpose. He knows what each of us can endure and will deposit in us the power to persevere and to be victorious. Every trial is different: the constant is the fact that God will never give us more than we can bear.

The months following August 2002, I felt like Elijah. God had wonderfully led His prophet in a glorious defeat of the prophets of Baal at Mount Carmel but immediately after that stunning victory he plummeted into depression under a threat from the wicked Queen Jezebel (**1 Kings 18 - 19:1-5-NIV**). Here I was, ecstatic that I had survived major surgery, but with the news that the tumor was back and another surgery was necessary, I fell into a state of depression. I had to delve into God's Word to encourage myself and contend with what Tommy Barnett called *"juniper blues"* in the book **Desert Experience.**

It was about this time that the diagnosis also changed. After the surgery in May 2002, the hospital had sent a small portion of the tumor overseas for further tests and their finding was that I had 'Aggressive Fibromatosis' and not 'Plexiform-Nuerofibroma.' (For further information see the End notes). The good news was that this kind of tumor was also non–cancerous even though it could behave as if it were cancerous.

There were times when this whole journey felt like an emotional purgatory and so journaling for me was like a catharsis. Here are some of my entries.

Journal entry September 3, 2002

......I must ask you to remember. I'm standing on your Word because I have nothing else to stand upon. I believe that You have healed my body and you are going to make right what is going wrong. You will give me a new body. I'm not just asking you because I'm feeling pain but because I have faith in you. I believe in you. You know me God and I'm standing on your promises. I want to please you. The writer to the **Hebrews** warns us: *"...without faith it is impossible to please God"* (11: 6 - NIV). And that's the prayer of my heart: to please only you.

God, no matter what is going on in my body I know You can fix it because You created me; You knew me when I was not yet formed in my mother's womb. If there is anything You want me to do just let me know. God, I want a conscious spirit so that I can be in tune with You. Continue to work in my life.

Regardless of what is happening to me, I am still going to be here praising Your name. Yes, sometimes I'm tempted to question You and Your ways. A part of me believes that I have done something wrong why this is happening to me but that's just the enemy. I know You are Omniscient, Omnipotent Omnipresent, Infallible and Immutable so, I am going to continue holding on to your Unchanging Hands.

Journal Entry September 30 2002

Hi God:

Just wanted to tell you how much I love You. I love You in spite of the pain I'm presently experiencing because I know You can fix it. Jesus you are all I need. I NEED You and only You. God I wrap myself in Your Word. I not only stand on them but I rest in them. God, Almighty, I believe only You...

All my life God, just take full control. God, use me and humble me in the process. Help me to remember who gets the glory always. God, help me through this. Hold my hands, hold both of them, hold me Jesus. God, when the manifestation of my healing comes (notice I say <u>when</u> not <u>if</u>) give me a new way to praise You...God place a hunger in my soul for You daily.

Journal entry October 30, 2002

This morning I come thanking you for another day. God, I'm in so much pain right now it isn't funny. God, I'm not complaining. I realize the many blessings I have in my life and I would never dare take it for granted. You said in your words that we should pour out our hearts to You and be honest before You. I am doing that this morning. God, I'm sick and tired of the pain. Part of me is thinking I'm ready for my eternal sleep but I'm not giving up on life. God, it's just that I am so tired of the pain. I want a body without pain...

The pain, Jesus, the pain!!! Stop the pain please!!! Yes, I'm worshipping You in the midst and thanking You for this fire but God I'm at my wits end. Every single day I'm in pain. God please stop the pain. I'm so tired of the pain. Please stop the pain!!! Please God...

I chose to include these journal entries to show how my emotions fluctuated dramatically as time progressed. At times, I wanted to scream at God because of the pain. It was always the pain that made me feel like I wanted to die. It was so overwhelming sometimes but in my heart I knew that I had to go through this process that God had allowed in my life and not doing so would mean that I failed this test. The motivation that kept me going was that I never wanted to let go of my relationship with Him.

The fact that God was with me, and my hope was in Him, kept me sane.

In November 2002, I discovered a small lump (inclusion cyst) on the left side of my neck, close to the area of the incision. I remember thinking, *"I would tell Dr. Irvine about it and he would just inject it with something and it would just disappear!!!"* So imagine my surprise when during one of my follow-up visits he told me that it would have to be removed surgically!!! I was now faced with the possibility of two surgeries, one to remove the re-growth of the tumor; and the other to remove this lump on the left side of my neck. With tears in my eyes I asked him if there were any other way to get rid of the lump. He told me *"No."*

This surgery was scheduled for Thursday, November 28, the only bright side to this surgery was that it could be done within one day without my being admitted to the hospital. I agreed to do the surgery as an out-patient, on the condition that by midday, I would be at home in bed recuperating. So, Dr. Irvine made the necessary arrangements.

I did not want anyone to accompany me because it would have been too distressing to see the worry or anxiety on their faces. My father objected but I tried to convince him that I would be okay. That didn't work. In the end, two close family friends accompanied me. I didn't really tell many persons about the surgery because it was a minor one and also I did not want to hear, *"Elloraine, you are doing another surgery!"*

By 9:00 o'clock on Thursday morning I was in the operating theatre. This surgery lasted just about an hour. It was a very painful experience. I felt successive injections into the incision in order to numb the area. It was plain horrible. Tears started to flow effortlessly.

I told the persons attending to me, *"Don't worry, the tears will soon subside; I am just mentally tired, that's all."* To my surprise, Dr. Irvine came by to see me. He ended up staying for most of the surgery. He held my hand and told me about his wedding, which was just his way of distracting me from focusing on the pain. I was so grateful for the fact that he was holding my hand and consoling me through this minor but very painful surgery. He is truly a compassionate person.

Immediately upon returning to the ward, I sprang off the gurney, and got dressed to leave. In the process of dressing, I caught a glimpse of my reflection in the mirror. My eyes were red and slightly swollen from crying and I couldn't believe the huge dressing on my neck!!! I guess the thought of attending church on Sunday was suddenly out of the question.

Dr. Irvine kept his promise because by midday I was at home in bed. Although I was feeling immense discomfort and pain, I was so relieved it was over.

Towards the end of the year 2002, the pain continued to assault my body but I was happy to be alive to spend another Christmas with my family and friends. The following journal entry gives you an idea of what was happening and how I felt.

Journal Entry December 30, 2002

God, my back is hurting me beyond comprehension. My left hand is cramped from this terrible pain. My back feels like it is splitting in two. My back, Oh God my back. Please touch my back Jesus!!!

The pain feels lethal... Sometimes I wonder what is really causing so much pain in my body. Why does it hurt so much to take a deep breath? It could not be from only a broken breast bone, could it? Sometimes I feel so mentally tired, my body feels so tired. I wonder sometimes when my strength or energy will snap. ..

The following year I learned how to better cope with the pain. I didn't cry out to God very often and say, *"Take me, Take me I want my eternal sleep. I can't bear this pain anymore!!!"* The truth was I got so used to the pain that at times it did not spiral me into the regular depth of frustration.

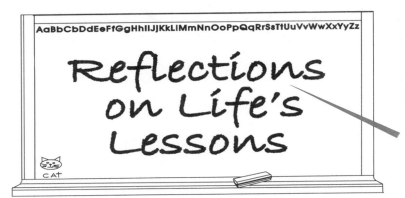

- If someone had told me that by the end of the year 2002 I would have been in an operating theatre three times I would not have believed them. By my plans, I should have been preparing for my wedding but, to quote Tommy Barnett and **"Desert Experience,"** again, *"Make your plans in pencil and give God the eraser."* We have to always be mindful that God's plan for our lives supersedes our own plans or desires. This was indeed what was happening to me. We have to trust God because He sees the big picture; the one that you and I are not able to see. He has everything in control and everything is done according to His divine plan.

Answers

As I returned to my seat
Unanswered questions engulfed my thoughts.
I tried to make sense of it all
But again, I was surrounded by the wall:
The unscalable, unbreakable,
Answers-unattainable,
Constricting, fear- inflicting wall.

I ponder and wonder if I'm futureless;
Friends and loved ones are clueless.
Each day I'm greeted by their sighs
For neither they nor I can answer the 'whys'.

They don't understand that even "in light of"
I'm encouraged to hold on "in spite of".
At this point I've almost lost my grip,
Each day feels like a downhill trip.

Whether I feel like it or not
I've realized life forces you to give it another shot

Tomorrow is a new day, the sun will shine
As people go about their daily lives.
Hold on!
No answers.
Hang in there!

In this world there will be troubles
now and forever more
And you must endeavor to endure.
You must be comforted by the thought
That God does only what He ought.
Trust Him though at times answers are not apparent
Remember as a problem solver He is excellent.
Patiently wait on Him to do
What He knows is best for you.

By Elloraine Lothian & Earle Stewart

My
Unexpected
Journey

Learning to Be Content

The year 2003 was a special one for me. With God's help my mentality changed and I decided to make the best of my circumstances. I have not been gainfully employed since 2002 and my medical bills were mounting. Both bank accounts were on "E" (empty). However, with the help of my cousin Lorna, I found innovative ways to enjoy myself and to find contentment and peace. Like the Apostle Paul, *"I have learned to be content whatever the circumstances."* (Philipians. 4: 11-NIV). I recalled the words of Tim Robbins in his role as Andrew 'Andy' Dufresne in the movie, The Shawshank Redemption, *"You get busy living or get busy dying."* Armed with my pain killers, I chose to get busy living.

Between April and August 2003, I lived like a tourist. I "owned" Jamaica's northcoast – the Caribbean's tourist Mecca! My favourite place in the world (until I visit Hawaii, Paris or the Fuji Islands) is Dunn's River Falls in Ocho Rios. I went there as many times as I could. I visited the Green Grotto Caves in Runaway Bay, relaxed at Island Village Shopping Centre in Ocho Rios and dined at an all-inclusive resort.

On one of my trips to Ocho Rios, I gained a new appreciation for my feet. It was a far distance from Island Village to the bus terminal and as I walked the intensity of the pain in my back became so overwhelming that I was tempted to complain. As I slowed my pace I saw a man with two long wooden legs, immediately tears stung my eyes. From then on the journey to the bus terminal was punctuated by the words, *"Thank you God for my feet; I can walk!"* For the rest of the day, I consciously continued to give God thanks.

I have always appreciated the simple rituals of life that we sometimes take for granted but I was reminded again that day how important they really are. It is no idle thing to say, *"If you want to see how blessed you are, just visit a hospital."*

I took each day as it came. If today seemed an intense day of pain, and it meant that I would cry all day, that's what I would do to cope. If it seemed to be a sighing day, then that is what I had to do to get through it. On the good days I never ceased giving thanks. But underneath it all, good or bad, there was a peace because God was with me and I knew that as long as I had Him with me I would make it through. Challenging days may be ahead but they will be challenging with Jesus by my side and that made it alright.

The year 2003 was indeed special. In addition to the things related before, I have learned that if I won the battle in my mind then I would make it and my body would just have to catch up with my spirit. I was reminded that God was the only one that could really give me peace, (real unfathomable peace). *What do I mean?* I could be scheduled for surgery tomorrow and the day before admission I would be at the beach sipping a virgin Pina Colada. That is just God's awesome peace.

On Wednesday, June 18, God used one of my friends, Tamika, to give me a word of comfort. *"I am a God of my promises. I'm going to use you and show people My greatness, how good I can be. I am a God of my Word."*

God will give words of comfort when one is going through difficult circumstances. Sometimes it is just the line of a song, or word of Scripture, or a phrase from a sermon. These times taught me that God knows exactly what I need and when I needed it. The word I got that Wednesday was fuel in my tank for several months. So, I reaffirmed in my spirit, *"Something good is going to come out of this. There is indeed purpose to all this even though sometimes I don't feel it or see it. This process must have a great reward in it."*

In July, I did an abdominal ultrasound and I received the news that I had multiple fibroids. I will never forget this particular incident because to this day I still laugh about it. While I was there gazing on the ultrasound monitor, I counted about six small tumors. Out of curiosity I asked the doctor who was examining me, *"How many fibroids are there?* She bluntly answered, *"I usually stop counting after four."* I had to resist the urge not to laugh hysterically. I guess a part of me was expecting her to be more compassionate and say, *"Miss*

Lothian, when there are so many I don't usually count them all."

In the midst of the possibility of another surgery, I had to deal with the news that I had multiple fibroids. One of my doctors advised me to have them removed because they could cause problems in the future. He said I should consider surgery to remove the fibroids after I did the surgery to remove the re-growth of the tumor. I remember thinking, *"Are you kidding me!!! You must be joking, right? Do another incision on this body? At this rate there won't be much of me left for the husband or even the three children I plan to have."*

I started seeking God's direction about the surgery to remove the tumor. In the process, I put aside thoughts about the multiple fibroids; that was a case by itself. I wasn't ready to deal with that; I had too much on my plate. I could feel the pressure mounting on me mentally. Later in the month, I experienced one of my "all-time lows". I did not understand what was happening. In addition to that, I was learning one of the most difficult emotional lessons known to man. I felt like I was an ideal patient for a psychiatric ward and it was only the grace of God that kept me.

By September, the pain became so intense that traveling became difficult. My excursions between April and August were a thing of the past. At least I enjoyed myself and I have the memories and the pictures to cherish. As the days passed and unanswered questions assailed my mind, I continued to journalize.

Journal Entry September 5, 2003

... God, do you really want me to do another surgery? I don't know what to do. I want to hear from you so desperately. I have no audible prayer left. I don't know what to pray anymore!!! I can't help myself; I have no strength left to do anything. God, did you hear me? I HAVE NO STRENGTH LEFT!!! I have lost the will to fight once more. Everything is just a mess right now.

God, what is it I'm supposed to be doing at this stage? God will you ever touch my body and make me "normal" again? Will I have to do a second major surgery to remove the tumor and get more cuts on my already depleted body? I mean, how can anybody in their right mind insist that I do another surgery...?

God Almighty, please help me I'm drowning here. I have no big prayer. It's just an imperfect Elloraine calling out to a perfect God. This is torture, God, I need your help!!!

God *did* answer my prayer for direction. Sometime in October, praying women came to my house and in the midst of their encouragement, by divine confirmation, I

Elloraine Lothian

was directed to go ahead and do the surgery. The tears that eluded me in the previous months started to flow once more. I cried and I cried and in between sobs I said, *"I'm alright, I'm alright. If He is okay with the surgery so am I."* That's all I needed, the assurance that God is with me on this.

On the morning of November 9, that momentous year, 2003, I was admitted again to the hospital. This is my journal entry on that occasion.

Journal Entry November 09, 2003

My admission to the hospital this time was special as I was in my own private room. There was closet space, a face basin and most of all privacy. It was too good to be true and I was grateful. In the spirit of thanking God for the little things and making the best of my situation, I was ecstatic because on previous occasions I didn't have a private room.

I was extremely calm and peaceful on the morning of the surgery. A divine peace settled in me that prepared me for the operation. At one point, I found myself browsing through a Vogue magazine. Not "appropriate" literature for a Christian going into major surgery! But I had no need to search the Scripture for consolation; my Father had already given it to me. That morning, to read my bible was only my Christian obligation.

The surgery would be done by an ENT surgeon; it was scheduled to last between three and five hours. Yes, there could be complications but I had no fear. God had given me such reassurance that I knew that I was relaxed going into the operating theatre. I promised the devil that I would smile on my way into the operating theatre and that it is the first conscious thing that I would do in the recovery room.

I entered the operating theatre early that morning, with my smile, and fell asleep about 8 o'clock. I awoke in the recovery room, with the smile I promised the devil; when I looked at the clock it was a few minutes after 2:00 pm. "Hallelujah, Hallelujah!!!!" By 3 o'clock, I was back in my room and it was time for "operation look good". With the help of one of the nurses I did look my best for my visitors later that evening.

I was told that the surgery was successful but they had to leave a small portion of the tumor because it was too close to an important nerve connected to my left hand. *"Wait a minute, my left hand, my precious ring finger!!!"* Sometime in the future I wanted to feel the ring that my 'Boaz' would place on it. So it was just fine with me that no damage was done to it. My left hand had already been weakened because of the tumor suppressing the nerve.

The following morning, the doctors told me I could go home. That was unbelievable. It was not normal for persons who had undergone major surgery to be released the next day. Looking back at the entire experience, God has just left me speechless. He has put this inexplicable joy in my soul; I can't imagine my life without Him.

The year ended with me feeling an overwhelming sense of gratitude just to be alive! Thank God! - Alive to see another Christmas.

I am sure I can do this

Cheers to life...Nats and I at the beach

A day at Island Village

At a formal function

AaBbCcDdEeFfGgHhIiJjKkLlMmNnOoPpQqRrSsTtUuVvWwXxYyZz

Reflections on Life's Lessons

CAT

- At first, when the doctors had suggested doing another surgery, I did not want to do it. However, after wrestling with my thoughts and delving into the Word of God, I found contentment. In addition, I received divine confirmation to do the surgery. Being a Christian for so many years, I knew Scripture tells us that we are not our own – **(1 Corinthians 6:19-CEV)** says, ***"…The Spirit is in you and is a gift from God. You are no longer your own."*** So, it was not about what *I* wanted. In response, I said, *"If God wants me to do another surgery it is okay` as long as He is leading."*

- In spite of the traumatic situation you may be experiencing get busy living. I know the temptation is there to live in the land of the *"Why me Lord"* syndrome but don't succumb. Learn to enjoy your life by doing simple rituals such as going to the beach, visiting a museum or just spending time with friends. Do what you have to do in order to keep the essence of your spirit alive.

Inside

When we are cast down
Hurled from side to side
By the happenings of the day
We are battered by the storms of life
Where will we ever get the strength to cope,
to continue, to last?
Inside

Things ought to get better
But they only escalate to the worst
The orgasm of sadness, depression, and frustration
No peace, no hope, no joy in any situation

There is a place on the Inside
That no human can reach
It's a place way deep down
Where a reservoir of hope dwells
Strength that defies description erupts
On the Inside
Renewed vigor, confidence to carry on
It's deep on the Inside

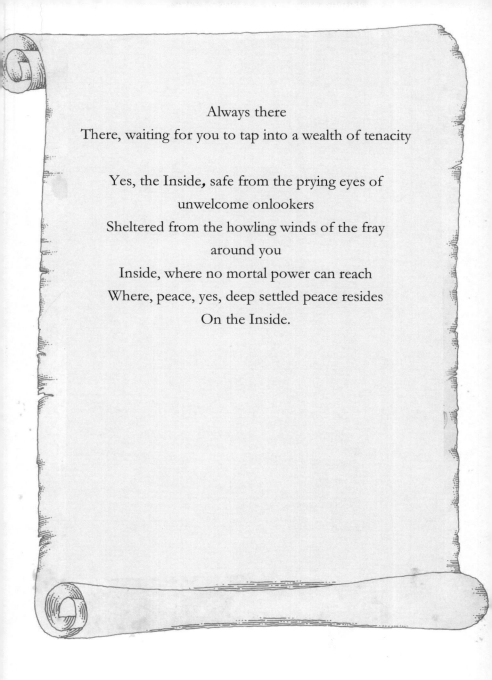

Always there
There, waiting for you to tap into a wealth of tenacity

Yes, the Inside, safe from the prying eyes of
unwelcome onlookers
Sheltered from the howling winds of the fray
around you
Inside, where no mortal power can reach
Where, peace, yes, deep settled peace resides
On the Inside.

My
Unexpected
Journey

Another Surgery?
I don't think so!!!

CHAPTER FIVE

One of the greatest lessons learned during 2003 was the fact that everything that God permits us to experience works out ultimately for our good. I no longer screamed, *"I AM NOT DOING ANOTHER SURGERY!"* but now calmly say, *"If it were up to me I would not do another surgery but if it is God's leading, then it is okay. He will give me the strength and peace to go through it. God's purpose must be accomplished in my life. It may not all make sense to me but He is God and I trust Him."* As the New Year unveiled itself I continued my journaling:

Journal January 19, 2004
God,
...Just want to affirm that you are my God and you mean so much to me. I love you so much, even though I don't tell you often enough. You are my world. You are the centre of my joy. You are my life. You are the air that I breathe. You are all I need in this life. You are my friend, my lover, and the essence of my being. I just love you dearly...There is no one in the world who loves me like you do. All I want to do is to live for you. You have been so good to me. I would be wicked if I complained. As long as I know I have you by my side I'll be alright...

In January 2004, I started experiencing hoarseness in my throat. It felt as if something was lodged in there and my voice began to sound different. Out of concern, I visited the ENT clinic on January 22 for an examination. One of the doctors suspected that there was a granuloma (a small nodule) on one my vocal chords and it would have to be removed surgically. My first reaction was to smile; I smiled for at least 10 seconds because I thought what I was hearing was simply a joke. The doctor asked me why was I smiling, and I told him that I was only trying to prevent myself from crying. I asked him where on my throat an incision would be made in order to remove the nodule. He told me there would be no visible incision. He explained that I would be put to sleep and an instrument would be inserted into my throat in order to sever the nodule.

I was elated because even though this would be my fifth surgery I wouldn't experience the trauma of another surgical incision. So, of course readily I asked, *"When do you want me to come in?" I thought to myself, "This one is easy. Hallelujah, no cut!!! No cut. I could break out dancing..."*

On January 30, I was back in the hospital to undergo this procedure to remove the nodule from my vocal cord.

Below is the journal entry highlighting my state of mind earlier that day.

Journal January 30, 2004

I am back in the hospital one more time after surgery on November 10, 2003. This time around I just asked my friend Dale to take me to the hospital. I really did not want any family members here for this one. It would be too much for them. Besides, I don't think this surgery is major or serious mainly because there will be no external incision. To be honest, it may sound crazy but I was excited to come back into the hospital just to prove to the devil that no matter what, I am coming out smiling. There is such a peace in my soul, it is indescribable.

Although this would be my fifth surgery I am going in smiling and I will come out of it grinning.
With God by my side, the devil is no match for me...

Later that day, the doctors gave me details about the surgery to be done, after which they did a Laryngoscopy (a procedure to intricately examine the larynx). Upon completing the examination, they informed me that there was no evidence of any nodule on my voice box. It took me a while to comprehend it, but I finally understood. God just performed His own miraculous healing! I returned to my bed ecstatic, I thanked God for coming through for me once more. I did my little pivot netball dance and I was packed and ready to go home.

I recalled attending a fasting service at my church prior to my hospitalization. At that meeting, persons prayed for me in a militant mode and declared many things over my life including, *"no more surgeries"* and they anointed me with consecrated olive oil.

When Carlie came that evening to visit, I said, *"Come let's go. We are going home."* He looked at me with a puzzled look on his face and I explained that the doctors said there was no need for an operation. This just showed me that God could also have prevented all the other surgeries but he allowed me to do them because they were all a part of His divine plan and purpose for my life.

After being discharged from the hospital, I continued to walk in my victory, giving God glory for the manifestation of His awesome power in my situation. Pain was bearable at this point but unfortunately, by April the chronic pain that I used to experience in my neck and back returned. This time it was accompanied by occasional cramps in my left hand. It was the Word of God that got me through the year. I also made it my priority to go to church whenever the doors were open. I had learned from my pastor Bishop, the Rev. Dr. W.A. Blair that you go to church on two occasions: when you feel like it and when you don't. I was in pain whether I was at home or not, so, I may as well go to church.

I noticed that some of my worst nights were usually on Saturdays, the day before my regular day of worship, and it was on those nights that I got little or no sleep. Sometimes, I would sit in church after a sleepless night and my body felt so weary that I would just whisper, *"My body may be in this chair but my spirit is running the aisle worshipping and declaring, I'm still here and I'm going to continue to be here. I'm going to keep showing up again and again. I have God, the Holy Ghost and Jesus on my side and I'm going to continue to believe God until my breakthrough comes."*

The severe intensity of the pain became encouragement for me to go to church. I had made up my mind that if I had to go to church on a gurney that was what I would do. I know it may sound crazy but it was my way of saying to the devil, *"The pain will never stop me."* It's all about winning the battle in your soul (the mind, the will and the emotions).

I came to understand and to truly appreciate the theology of the body, soul and spirit, which states that man is a spirit living in a body and possessing a soul. My body was sick but my spirit was fine. My soul was where the real battle took place; that's where I had to win the war against depression, complaining and murmuring. With God's help I will win the battle raging in my soul.

So, I learned to live by the strength of my spirit...that's what carried me through 2004. During that year I studied different versions of the Bible so that I could find a translation that would make the Word sink deep into my soul and strengthen my mind. Another lesson that I have learned was God *is* truly my source and He knows exactly what I need and when I needed it. He is truly an 'on time God.' There were rare moments when a day would pass and I didn't have food to eat. I could tell you many stories of how God came through for me in terms of supplying my needs but I will just share two testimonies:

During August 2004, I was at the shopping mall, I had JA$1000. Before going to the mall, I felt depressed because I could not find a suitable top to wear. Due to my financial status, I did not have enough money to spend on clothes. I challenged God right there and then to do something for me. I said, *"God, your Word says we should not worry about clothes or food. Well, you know how many things I need but this money can do so much and no more. So, I'm going to buy myself two blouses and trust you to provide for the rest of my needs."* This challenge was based on a word from Paul to the **Philippian** church family: ***"And my God will meet all your needs according to his glorious riches in Christ Jesus"*** **(4:19 –NIV)**. I was standing on that verse.

I purchased two blouses for JA$800 and I had JA$200 left to pay for transportation to go home. Later that day, God's answer came when one of my church sisters called to tell me that she had JA$2000 to give me. I smiled. *"Now that's what I'm talking about!!! God you will certainly take care of all my needs."*

Another case of God's provision that stands out vividly in my mind was on a particular Sunday, when all I had was the bus fare to go to church. I did not feel like going but I went anyway. When the church service ended, my internal dialogue with God went something like this, *"God, only you and I know that all I had was the bus fare to come here, so, now it's up to you to get me home."*

On my way out of the church, someone intercepted me and told me that one of my 'mothers in Christ' wanted to see me. I went in search of her and when I found her she said, *"Elloraine do you know how long I have this for you?"* She handed me JA$1000. I held her with both hands and looked directly at her eyes and said, *"Believe me when I tell you that today is the day that I should have received this money, not last week or two weeks ago but today."* I was laughing hysterically. I chartered a taxi to take me home. I sat in air-conditioned comfort smiling as I traveled home in style.

The resurgence of the chronic pain in my neck and back since April 2004 was maddening. I kept in touch with Dr. Irvine on a regular basis to inform him about what was happening to me. While he respected my desire not to do another surgery, he advised me to do a CT scan to determine if the tumor was growing back. On November 9, I did the scan which confirmed its regrowth. This was the same date the previous year that I was admitted to the hospital to do the fourth surgery. Now, exactly one year later I had to deal with the news that the tumor was back. It felt like a nightmare that just would not go away.

The next day I received an awesome prophetic word from the Lord through my friend Tina. Everything that was my heart's desire was prophesied to me. The word declared, *"...it was a new season in my life, God would fulfill all my desires, He would restore me and my healing had begun..."* This confirmed to me that God was working by His timing. It was no coincidence that I got this word at this time. God was up to something and the prayer of my heart was that I would not miss it.

By the second week in December things took a turn for the worse. I began to experience terrible pain on the left side of my head that I had never felt before. During this difficult time, one of my spiritual mothers, Dale, became my 2:00 a.m. prayer partner. It was precisely at 2:00 a.m. in the morning that the headaches would start and they were brutal. As a result of these, I had many sleepless nights and I thank God for Dale who stayed up with me during those hours.

It was at this point that I felt that the fiery trial was most intense. I literally felt like I was losing my mind. I can vividly remember that between Wednesday, December 15, and Saturday December 18 I did not get any sleep. I cried out to God and told Him I could not bear the pain especially when my body was starved for sleep. It was then that I realized the value of undisturbed sleep. I told God that the only gift I wanted for Christmas was undisturbed sleep. He granted my request.

I recognized that the devil wanted me to doubt God and the words of comfort that I had received from Him the previous month, but He could not break my faith or my spirit. My spirit was still strong even though my body was frazzled. At this point, two small lumps were protruding at the side of my neck.

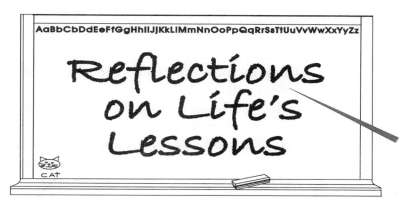

- Do you trust God enough to show up and do as He says even though it does not make sense to your natural mind? God can heal you before you do any surgery but He, at times, tests how flexible you are in His hand.

- God is truly our source. He knows exactly what we need and when we need it. His Word is true. Once we stand on it and trust Him to provide for our every need He will. God always takes care of His children. Where He guides, He provides so have faith in His Word.

- As Christians, there are some challenging situations that we will encounter and we will earnestly pray for God to deliver us or take them away. However, I have learned that sometimes God will not take the situation away but He will give us the grace to endure it and to come out victorious. There are some trials that He will take you *through,* not out of. If God should take us out of every situation or trial that we experience, we would never grow as Christians and mature in our faith and confidence in Him. There are some experiences though difficult that are essential to build our character and make us more Christ-like. Scripture states: *"...We also rejoice in our suffering, because we know that suffering produces perseverance; perseverance character; and character hope"* (Romans 5:3-4 – NIV).

- Sleep is vital to both spiritual and physical health. I did not realize how true this was until I could not sleep. I implore you; give thanks for the blessing of sleep.

- It is so important that we understand that the real battle takes place in our mind. It is therefore necessary that we feed our soul (mind, will and emotions), constantly with God's Word so that we can win the war against depression, complaining and murmuring. If we win the battle in our mind it will only be a matter of time before we overcome our challenges.

Another Operation

Oh God, another operation
But this time it's joy and jubilation
Oh boy, oh joy, I rejoiced no more cuts
However, we know at the peak of elation
there is always a but
I remembered the firm declaration of my
sisters and brothers
That for surgeries there will never be another

No matter how it looks like I'm bruised,
battered and dying
The devil is gonna see me smiling
This time around I didn't even need family
just a caring friend
God covered so much all I needed was
one person to attend

Yes, I most joyously approached this operation
With a childish unrestrained jubilation
I saw opportunity in chaos
Or perhaps I was merely adventurous
No! I was lucid I was fully aware
This was my stratagem to be the devil's nightmare
I was examined and all were amazed just astounded
To realize no nodule could be located
they were confounded

After that victory
the devil was furiously determined
That in the other confrontations I would not win
Poor devil
He doesn't understand
I'm a victor, I will always stand

I may lose a battle but not the war
Because I will always be God's shinning star
He tried but again he failed
Refused to realize that he cannot prevail
No matter the many surgeries no matter how long
God to you alone I will always belong.
My love for you surpasses any situation
Thank you God for cancelling this operation.

Earle Stewart

My
Unexpected
Journey

Giving up is not an Option

By 2005, pain was no longer an issue. I had learnt over the years to endure it and as such, I became a veteran of pain. Although I was implored by my doctors to consider the possibility of another surgery I flatly refused. I was holding on to my prophetic word of November 10, 2004. Also, I just did not have the peace to do another surgery. Yes, the pain was horrible and it seemed like the pain killers were not effective. My body had now become immune to them.

The principle of surviving by the moment was how I lived. If I were to record some of my night time experiences it would be something like this: for the first couple of hours I would pace the floor, at times I would cry, then I would lie on the floor with pillows to try and get some sort of 'comfort' in pain.

Thankfully, there were other times when I slept on the wings of prayer.

As the tumor was protruding noticeably from the side of my neck, I had to deal with the constant reaction from the public. It seemed like it came out of nowhere but in reality it had been steadily growing since the last surgery. As the pain intensified, I was instructed by Dr. Irvine to do another CT scan. Since I had refused to do another surgery, the scan was necessary to help him monitor the growth of the tumor. So, in June 2005, the CT scan was done and the result was:

> The tumor has now expanded in all directions. It now extends from the level of the voice box down to the arch of the aorta (the main blood vessel of the heart). In the neck, it lies behind the carotid artery (which controls the blood supply to most of the brain on the left side) and pushes it forward. All other structures in the left side of the neck are pushed toward the front and the right. As the mass enters the chest cavity it completely encases the carotid artery and partially encases the left subclavian artery (the blood supply to the left arm and rest of the left side of the brain). The vein from the left side of the head, neck, and left arm also lies to the front of the tumor. The artery supplying the right upper limb and the right side of the brain also lies to the front of the tumor.

> The left carotid artery (the arterial supply to the left side of the brain) is pushed to the front. There is now erosion of another vertebra in the chest as a result of the expansion of the tumor.

The **Psalmist** David's affirmation *"My times are in thy hand..."* (31:15a-KJV) became my mantra and carried me through the year. My times are in God's hands and it does not matter how my body looks or feels. I did however feel like I was not going to survive this tumor based on how my body felt. It seemed death was more appealing than life and that the best thing God could do was to take me home. But my heart was persuaded that His purpose would be fulfilled. I had received too many prophetic words that, *"I shall not die, but live, and declare the works of the Lord."* (Psalm 118: 17-KJV).

At times, my chest would tighten as if I were an asthmatic and I had difficulty breathing. I started experiencing shortness of breath whenever I did simple tasks. I felt as if a bulldozer was parked on my chest. The first time I had experienced this feeling was after the biopsy in March 2002. By May 2005, the quality of my voice began to deteriorate. I sounded as if I were constantly hoarse. The doctors suspected that the tumor was resting on a nerve in the area of my voice box, causing the quality of my voice to change. However, I still maintained that I had no peace about doing another surgery and God gave me the strength to endure the remaining months of that year in spite of what was happening to my body.

There were many thoughts that kept me going through the year; thoughts like, *"What does the end of this journey look like?"* Of course, giving up was not an option. I had come too far having survived purely by God's help since 2002 when I was first diagnosed with the tumor. It made no sense to even contemplate giving up now. And the million dollar question arose, *"Give up and do what?"* God was on my side and somehow I would make it. After several years of going through this trying ordeal:

- I was thoroughly trained in shedding tears.

- I was thoroughly trained in bearing excruciating pain.

- I was thoroughly trained in battling mental despair.

- I was thoroughly trained in living by the principle that God is my only Source.

- I was thoroughly trained in surviving by the moment in spite of financial challenges.

- I was thoroughly trained in weathering feelings of hopelessness, weariness, and distress.

- I was thoroughly trained in having sleepless days and nights.

Even though I was going through all these things I knew that there were persons who were experiencing more serious and life-threatening illnesses or challenges. There were persons battling cancer, malignant brain tumors, Leukemia, HIV virus, AIDS, uncommon illnesses or severe deformities. I was thankful for this insight and counted my many blessings. This helped me not to give in to the temptation to complain.

There were times when I thought, *"Is there something that I should be doing that I'm not doing? Am I lacking in faith? Am I not praying and believing enough?"* In spite of all these unanswered questions, I held on to my conviction that God does all things according to His purpose, and so the situation will ultimately work out for my good. **Romans 8:28- NLT** put it in perspective for me: ***"And we know that God causes everything to work together for the good of those who love God and are called according to His purpose for them."***

A corollary to the foregoing is Peter's reminder to *"... **not forget this one thing, dear friends: With the***

Lord a day is like a thousand years, and a thousand years are like a day" (2 Peter 3:8-NIV).

When I read that verse I would be lying if I told you that I found it comforting. This meant that four years of suffering would be like seconds or minutes according to God's divine calendar. God created time for our benefit and we must accept the truth that He is never in a hurry in accomplishing His purpose in our lives. I beseeched Him to help me to learn and understand that He is an 'on-time God.'

I have seen many crisis situations resolved during the years that I have been believing for my complete healing. I vividly remember a crisis experienced by one of my sisters in Christ, Mrs. Edna Atkinson. Her granddaughter was diagnosed with a liver condition which required a transplant. The church family prayed desperately for her situation for approximately one year. God answered our prayers and she got the transplant. Presently, she is doing very well. Instances like these help to build my own faith and give me the courage to **"...*wait till my change comes.*" (Job 14:14 – KJV)**

At times, I had a great desire for a family of my own but because of this illness that was on hold. However, I still believe God that I will not always be on 'planet single' and childless.

Elloraine Lothian

Pensive thoughts as the year
2005 comes to a close

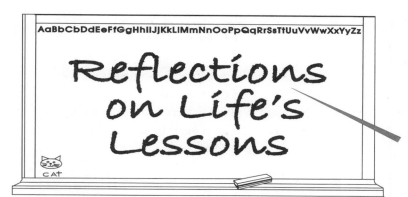

- I have observed that for some persons the longer they endure a valley experience their faith and trust in God becomes stronger. Consequently, they believe that something awesome is ahead. In my own situation, I kept telling myself that there is purpose in my suffering. That is why giving up is not an option.

- Friends, I know the temptation might be there to give up but, please, don't! Hang in there and fight! There is hope...you can make it through these challenging times. In my own situation, I am convinced that there will be great reward for this period of my life. **Hebrews 10:3-NIV** encouraged me, ***"So do not throw away your confidence; it will be richly rewarded."*** Remember Joseph and all his struggles? In the end God made him prosperous for all he endured **(Genesis 37-35-KJV)**. Job also hung in there; in the end God gave him double for his trouble

Trust Me

What do you do when you can't make sense
of the nonsense?
When the human mind is shattered into a thousand pieces
As pain, sorrows and grief seep in and destroy all hope
God says,
trust me

Your soul is crippled
You no longer see the need to live.
Tears are inadequate to express the hurt
on the inside
How do I even imagine going on?
You tell yourself this can't be happening!
No! No! No! No! Oh, God No!
And still a voice reassures,
'trust me.'

I must have done something wrong for this
tragedy to come my way!
Yes! That's it!
I'm being punished for some wrong that
I've committed
But still I don't deserve the magnitude of this pain
Yet deep down on the inside
He echoes,
"trust me I know what I'm doing."

Don't tell me to trust you!
How can I trust you?
I don't even know who you represent anymore!!!
I can't trust you
I won't trust you
But again you say, *'trust me...trust me'*...

My
Unexpected
Journey

My Divine Encounter

The first time I saw Paula White on Christian television was in October 2002. The message she delivered was entitled, *"Destined but Delayed."* As she spoke she was literally scraping me off the floor because at that time, my faith had hit rock bottom and it needed re-energizing. It was a timely message; a message of hope. I hung on to her every word. I wrote down something she distinctly said, *"God's purpose will stand. God says don't pay attention to what it looks like now."* This message helped me to enlarge my vision of who God really is. This was indeed a divine encounter. It reinforced in my mind Paul's words to the **Ephesian** brethren **(3:20-AMP)** which I have quoted many times:

97

> *Now to Him Who, by (in consequence of) the [action of His] power that is at work within us, is able to [carry out His purpose and] do superabundantly, far over and above all that we [dare] ask or think [infinitely beyond our highest prayers, desires, thoughts, hopes, or dreams]...*

The two words in the verse that really grabbed me are *'dare'* and *'superabundantly.'* I want to dare God for some superabundant blessings.

After hearing that message, I became devoted to listening to her messages. Through her teaching of the Word my faith in the Lord has grown and I have been led to a new appreciation for the Word. Scriptures that I may have overlooked, God has used her to nudge me to study and dissect them; I have received revelatory knowledge that has enhanced my spiritual development.

As Paula White Ministries is located in Tampa, Florida, I purposed in my heart to attend her church on my next visit to my sisters who live in close proximity to her church. So, I waited anxiously for the opportunity to go to Florida but God had a different plan; He was about to blow my mind!

In July 2004, while attending a regular Sunday morning service, I received a flier promoting the "Word Alive Women's Conference" to be held in Jamaica on July 22 – 24. The speakers who were scheduled included none other than Paul White. Even more amazing was the fact that the conference would take place at my church – Portmore New Testament Church of God. I could hardly believe it!!! I stared at the flier for a long while, doubting that Paula White was not only coming to Jamaica but to my church!!! I saw it in writing but still could not believe it. I kept saying to myself, *"...Paula White is coming to my church...no, this cannot true...* " But it was true.

On July 24, 2004, I was actually seeing Pastor Paula White in *my* church!!! At approximately 8:25 p.m. she began her sermon entitled, *"Have You Read My Resume?"* My eyes, my ears, my full attention were focused on her to receive every word. As she spoke it was as if she came to Jamaica just to minister to me. God used her to give me clarity and meaning concerning these trying years of my life. One thing she said that continues to reverberate in my mind was that, *"I came to Jamaica to give you understanding concerning the process that you have been going through...You have been challenged because you have been chosen...God is not going to give you a word, you are the sermon..."*

Following the Paula White encounter I wrote in my journal:

Journal Entry July 26, 2004

... She spoke under the anointing. She spoke with power and authority. There was a point in the service where the Holy Ghost just took over the place. I remember hollering like I've never done in a very long time. As I hollered, I told God I still believed that this pain would end one day. "It's not going to last forever...God; I believe that you are going to do something awesome in my life. It was not just coincidental that I attended this conference. God, show me your manifested presence. There is indeed purpose in this illness.

"God, in the end I know that you will get the glory. Persons will be amazed at what you are going to do in my life at the end of this process. Thank you Lord for using this conference to increase my faith..."

From that moment on I started to believe God for unimaginable things. My faith level rose to unbelievable proportions. I began to believe for things I normally wouldn't and to use the Word to build my faith, continuing what the Paula White encounter had started. I began to pray exceptional prayers. It was as if I were learning all over again how awesome and powerful God, the Creator of the universe, really is! I came to truly understand the words that came to **Jeremiah**, *"Behold I am the Lord, the God of all flesh: is there any thing too hard for me?"* **(32:27-KJV)**

Today, there is nothing that I am
God. I just simply say, *"God, I hav*
(that's the possible part) now you c
God, please enlarge my mind. Go
the mistake of limiting you. I wan
you have for me on this earth. I do no
heaven and see many things that I could have
but didn't because I did not have the faith to receive
God, please, do not let me limit you. Rather, help me to
appropriate the words of your prophet **Jeremiah**, **'*Call***
unto me, and I will answer thee, and shew thee great
and mighty things, which thou knowest not" (33:3–KJV).

Reflections on Life's Lessons

- Paula White's visit to my church proved to me that God can and will indeed do beyond that which we can imagine. Here I was with my limited thinking believing that I had to go to Florida to have an encounter with this spiritually dynamic woman of God, when God Himself, was simply saying, *"Elloraine, I can bring Paula White to your church here in Jamaica."* How many times have we limited God by our way of thinking? God wants us to ask Him for 'superabundant blessings' He wants us to have 'daring faith' to believe that He can do the unimaginable.

- God is always willing to do the extraordinary in our lives, yet our minds cannot perceive it, and so we don't ask Him. I thank God that experience has taught me to trust Him fully because there are no boundaries to what He can do in our lives. Give Him the chance…pray exceptional prayers and expect exceptional answers. .

Enlarge My Mind

This is my prayer to You
My Lord and My King
Make me to know that I can ask for anything
Don't let me think of You as in times past and days of old
When all I did was limit you in my soul.
Don't let me see as far as
my pea-sized mind can envision
When all you want to do is to stretch and to
broaden my vision.
God, there is so much more you can do in my life
If only I would let go of my daily struggles in this fight
And allow you to enlarge my mind.

God, increase the level of my faith in You
Stretch it to the very breadth of You
Teach me how to dare to dream and to
superabundantly imagine
God with your mind guiding mine
we could do so much damage.
Timely remind me that you can out do any plans,
hopes or desires I possess
God in you there is always success
Help me not to limit you by any past glories
I might have had

Lord, you have the world in the palm of your hand
Oh Lord, I choose to believe that you
can enlarge my mind.

Lord, I know and believe that you can do the impossible
Because You are God, the All-Powerful, Untamable
You made man from the dust
If only in you I would continually trust
Create opportunities Lord to help my faith in you to grow
Knowing that no good thing from me will you withhold
King of Kings, Lord of Lords, Architect of the universe
The Creator of time
Can you please enlarge this mind of mine?

Lord, this is my humble request
Knowing you will always give me the best
I won't be satisfied until
I see my life through Your eyes
I vehemently, adamantly refuse Satan's lies.
Yes, that old devil wants to poison my soul
But God I know that you are still in control
Everlasting God, Creator of the ends of the earth
I thank you in advance
Because I know with you I always have a second chance
It's just a matter of time
As I know you will enlarge this mind of mine.

My
Unexpected
Journey

Tribute to my Friend Melissa

In this chapter I introduce to you my friend Melissa Hunt. She changed my life dramatically during the short time that I knew her. A re-committed Christian, Melissa shared her life in many ways including writing a column in *The Outlook Magazine*. (A Sunday Gleaner publication). Our lives intersected in October 2002 while I was recuperating from major surgery that I had done in May of that year. She was introduced to me by her aunt and adopted mother, Mrs. Dolly Byrd. I was flattered and felt particularly grateful and blessed when Mrs. Byrd said she wanted Melissa and I to meet because she felt I would be an inspiration and a source of strength to her. God really knows how to put angels in our lives at the right time.

After meeting her she became my intimate stranger. I felt comfortable sharing my story with her. I showed her the photos taken during my surgery in May 2002. She looked at each of them, then stared at me and shook her head in disbelief. She told me that I was a strong person to have endured all of that. *"The God [Holy Spirit] who dwells in me is the one with all the strength...not me."* I responded.

She then had the courage to tell me her story. To say I was dumbfounded would not adequately describe what I felt after hearing her experience. I left her company that day wondering what I would have done if I were the one diagnosed with AIDS, with T cells count of four at age 22. It is said that an AIDS patient with T cells count of less than 200 would be seriously ill, hospitalized or dead but Melissa was alive and looked quite healthy. I guess she was an "AIDS Miracle." As I contemplated how I would have felt if I were in her position, I began to thank God that my struggles were 'small potatoes' compared to Melissa's. It is true that we often think our cross is unbearable until compared to someone else's. You will then realize that you are truly blessed. Melissa reinforced that for me and I thanked God for all my blessings.

So my resolve, even though I never expressed it verbally, was that I would be a friend to Melissa for as long as she needed me. I would be there to support her until the end of her journey. Melissa truly helped me to put my struggles on the back burner because here was someone who was going through something far worse than I could ever imagine.

I spoke about my "camera-ready smile" in a previous chapter, but, really, if ever there was someone with such a smile it was Melissa. And very often the smile would burst forth into infectious laughter - she could certainly laugh! That's one of the things that bonded us quickly; we both knew and valued the importance of laughter. At times, Melissa and I would laugh so hard, until tears would fill my eyes and I would have to hold my chest for fear that the metal clips would burst open.

For approximately one year Melissa and I were inseparable. I would accompany her to medical appointments and clinic visits. I would sit with her, hold her hands and comfort her. In addition, Melissa and I shared some special moments. The lessons learnt during those times continue to be a source of strength for me.

On one particular occasion, I was on a herbal program to see if changing my diet drastically would help to stop the re-growth of the tumor. I had to take more than ten large herbal capsules per day. Melissa herself was on medication and at times she got frustrated having to take so many tablets. So, in trying to teach her not to complain and to make the most of an unpleasant task, I told her that we could take our tablets at the same time. As we took each one, we alternately made jokes about how the tablets looked and the things they reminded us of. For the next 5-10 minutes we were in stitches. We laughed so hard we could hardly breathe. From that day onwards, I never heard Melissa complain about her medication. She eventually came to understand that complaining makes an unpleasant task worse but if we change and have a positive attitude then the situation will not be as bad as it seems.

As it was Melissa's strong conviction that the Lord had called her to educate and speak to her generation about HIV/AIDS, she undertook many speaking engagements at various institutions. Thorkild (a friend of ours) and I accompanied her to one particular speaking engagement. I remember it very well because during this time Melissa's health had begun to seriously deteriorate. She even contemplated cancelling her presentation but she said she didn't want to miss the opportunity to save someone from contracting this dreaded disease. So, with the little strength she had left she went to address the group of teenagers she was scheduled to meet.

This was the first time I saw her crying publicly and it broke my heart. I was not surprised to find myself shedding a few tears as well. In that moment, words failed me in expressing how proud I was of her.

One of the principles that Melissa and I both embraced was, *"you may be going through the fire but you don't have to smell like smoke."* So we made it our priority to always look our best at all times. In my own case, I had to learn to 'dress up' because with a large scar and a tumor that was protruding from the left side of my neck, I needed to make myself look like a diva at all times. It was my way of diverting the many stares away from my neck to my other God-given assets such as my platinum smile. Whenever Melissa dressed for her speaking engagements, it was as if she were stepping off the pages of a fashion magazine. She loved silver jewelry and select pieces would adorn the outfit, usually her favorite color—white.

Melissa's health began to deteriorate in October 2003. The process was rapid and in November she left the island for Trinidad & Tobago to seek help for a brain infection. My fourth surgery was done around this time and I was recuperating so I did not see her before she left. We spoke on the telephone and I told her, *"I'm sorry that I have to say goodbye to you over the telephone but I'll see you when you get back."* The next time I saw Melissa was in a casket.

On the day I heard of Melissa's death I was on my way to the ENT clinic for a routine follow up visit. At that moment my mind went blank. I remained in that state for several days.

Melissa had made me promise that I would write her remembrance and read it at her home-going. I was able to keep the first part of the promise, but not the second; her friend Keisha, who assisted me in writing the remembrance, read it on my behalf.

"Excerpt from Melissa's Remembrance"

In one of her articles written for The Gleaner's Outlook Magazine dated November 17, 2002, she wrote, "God had given me the strength and courage to speak openly about my illness and to give encouragement to those infected and affected by this disease. I would hate to go to my grave knowing that someone could have been encouraged by something I said or did, but I was too busy to even notice."

So, through tear-filled eyes she boldly spoke to her audience about her illness, capturing at that moment what would be her mission for the remaining years of her life.

Once Melissa was available she would be found sharing her experiences with groups at churches, schools, or corporate companies across the island, even if she were not in the best of health.

It was obvious that there was something exceptionally special about Melissa. When she spoke she was down–to-earth and appeared almost angelic. She would always capture the attention of her audience whenever she spoke about HIV/AIDS and how she coped with the disease. After each presentation, Melissa was sometimes the last person to leave the room as attendees would gather to talk, touch or embrace her. It would seem that everyone wanted to meet and interact with this young woman with her signature platinum smile.

Never once did she blame anyone for her illness. She accepted her reality with courage and in God's strength. She tried to make the best of her circumstances in spite of the difficulties experienced by persons who had to live with HIV/AIDS. It is said that adversity does not build character it reveals it [Anonymous]. This disease has truly revealed the pure honesty, strength and beauty that Melissa possessed. She is remembered for her bright smile. She spoke so much into action through her life. She wanted to be loved and wanted to give love in return. Has anyone ever studied the flight of a dove? A feeble creature yet it flies with grace and great distance...that was Melissa.

In closing, Melissa touched more persons in the last 18 months of her life than at any other time. It is said that life is not about counting the years but making the years count [Anonymous]. Melissa did just that – she made her years count. There is no denying her presence but it is difficult to accept her absence.

The best we can do is to pass on the legacy that Melissa has left behind. Live each day as if it were our last because we never know what tomorrow will bring. Make sure when it's your time to die that's all you have to do.

P.S. Melissa, please keep a seat beside you in heaven for me. We have to hang out in heaven and take pictures and share more laughter. I miss you so much. We love you to pieces.

In one of the many articles Melissa wrote for *The Outlook Magazine,* she spoke about our friendship. It appeared in the issue of February 16, 2003 under the title, "Good friends are better than pocket money," The excerpt from this article which appears below, is not for self-praise, I have included it because her words are a testimony that my commitment to be a genuine friend standing with her until the end had been fulfilled. She had indeed recognized my purpose in her life through our friendship.

Excerpt from the article entitled, "Good friends are better than pocket money."

"A couple of months ago, the Lord blessed me with a special friend. When I first met Elorraine, I never thought we would become such good friends or that she would play such an important role in my life. But now every day I look forward to seeing or hearing from her. Though she is not HIV positive, she has her fair share of hardships but she does not let that take away from her bubbly personality. She is one of the kindest persons I have met, she always has a smile and a kind word for everyone. I have learnt so much from her in the short time we have known each other. She has taught me how to be happy and content despite my situation and to live life to the fullest. Elorraine has been like a sister to me, she is there for me in good and bad times and she has a way of making sense of the most complicated situations. She would always say, "Ah mi chile, God knows what he is doing," and not without a smile.

What I like most about Elorraine is she pays no attention to the fact that I have AIDS. She is not my friend out of sympathy, but because she genuinely cares about me.

I spent the better part of the week reflecting on how gracious God has been to me, sending Elorraine into my life has certainly been much more than a blessing."

In the article, she spelt my name incorrectly but the most important thing about this article is that it testifies of how God can use two unlikely people to positively impact each other even in times of adversity.

Through my relationship with Melissa I got to know Mrs Byrd quite well. I was impressed with her Christian approach and her love for Melissa which led me to ask her for a contribution to this chapter. This was her response:

"Melissa was the daughter that we had always wanted. She was really my niece (my sister's only child). She affectionately called me 'Mommy' or Auntie Dolly. Melissa was 17 years old when my sister took her to England. She stayed in England for approximately four years and during that time we did not communicate with each other.

When Melissa returned to Jamaica and she re-entered our lives, our love bonded us together as a family. We were just settling down to the idea of being a family when we were torpedoed with the devastating news; Melissa was diagnosed with full-blown AIDS. It made me fall helplessly into the arms of God. I felt as if I was in a maze, not sure which direction to go or how to react. After a while, I plummeted into depression. All I saw was "death." I knew nothing about the virus only how one could get infected.

One year before we received this tragic news, the Lord laid it on us, through a group of women from Portmore Covenant Community Church, to reach out to persons who were living with HIV at the "Lord's Place," a home operated by Father Richard Ho-Lung and The Brothers of the Poor. This was my first experience dealing with persons living with this disease. Today, I look back and thank God in spite of all that has happened; because the time spent visiting the Lord's Place was really God's way of preparing me for that which would confront our own family.

It was really hard on us as a family, especially, when people became aware of Melissa's illness. I guess I was the rock in the family, who did not care what anyone thought about us. I had to be the fence around her to protect her from the insensitive words of others.

There were times when I would lock myself in my room and cry because I did not want her to see me when I crumbled to pieces overwhelmed by the situation. Later, I found out that she did the very same thing. I guess in some ways we both wanted to be strong and brave for each other. The difficulty of dealing with Melissa's illness brought me closer to the Lord. We received support from some persons but we were disappointed by others.

At times, I was very angry with some persons, especially Christians, who were afraid to come to my house. There were some who stopped eating with us and this made me furious because in times past my house was "the place" to be if you wanted a meal. The Lord had to teach me that everyone had their own fears and that not everyone was able to deal with this situation the way I did and so I became more understanding and patient.

Melissa, being a born again Christian before her illness, was determined to follow Jesus and to fulfill what she believed the Lord had called her to do. Her mission was to educate others about this dreaded virus, especially young people of her age group.

Being a peer educator really strengthened her. Her daily planner would be filled with appointments to address different groups of people all over Jamaica. As a mother, I was so proud of my HIV–positive daughter, and that love just kept on pouring out of me in abundance. It was this love that kept our family together even during the trying times, for example, the many hospital visits, the pneumonia, the fever, the vomiting and the diarrhea that came with the illness. I am grateful that the Lord placed people in our lives to help us to deal with the difficult times.

Melissa died one year and eight months after being diagnosed with AIDS. The last few days before her death were the most difficult. I did not notice that Melissa was dying because I was in denial but everyone around me saw that her life was slowing slipping away.

As the illness continued its onslaught on her body, she developed a brain infection. This caused her speech to change drastically. Her movement was that of a frail old woman and she was as light as a feather. It was a tradition for all us–my husband, myself, Melissa and Matthew, our twelve year old son, to huddle together on my bed to sleep. These times were no exception. It was as if by being together we could prevent the disease from taking Melissa's life. I remember secretly smiling to myself and thanking God for a king-size bed.

Melissa left for Trinidad and Tobago in November 2003. This was organized and paid for by the Red Cross of Jamaica, who offered to help with the treatment for her brain infection. Melissa died six days after her arrival in Trinidad and Tobago.   I still experience a sense of trauma whenever I remember the telephone call with the news of her death.

Melissa was very strong on what she wanted for her home-going: *"I want no black and white, only bright colours. I want lots of flowers and praise and worship songs. I don't want my home-going to be boring, Auntie Dolly."*

Melissa finally got her healing.   She went home to rest. Melissa, my dear, I love you endlessly - in life and in death. I miss you terribly.

Other friends of Melissa also wanted to pay tribute; I have included contributions from two of them.

Thorkild Lote (Friend from Norway)

Many people, both Jamaicans and Norwegians, asked me how Melissa became such a dear friend of mine. I'm not sure why they ask. Maybe it's because I tell people I did not make that many friends while I was in Jamaica.

I am still asked the same question and I respond the same way. We liked each other. We made room for each other. Luckily, by pure coincidence, we happened to be working on the same project and so we spent a great deal of time together.

That's how we got to know each other. I would list her personality traits: her warmth, her smile, her astonishing strength, her eagerness to help others, as some of the reasons why we were such good friends. After only knowing her for three or four months, I miss her as if she was someone I had known all my life. It's not because of any particular reason, I just do.

Shussharrah Hamilton (Friend from Jamaica)

Melissa and I had been friends for approximately five years. However, we became really close after about three years of knowing each other. She revealed to me, while we were at a church retreat in 2002, that she had been infected with the HIV virus. When she told me I shrugged nonchalantly. At that time, the reality and the weight of her words never really hit home. It's as if I was in denial.

After that conversation, I purposed in my mind to get to 'know' Melissa, to really understand who was this young woman. During our many conversations, we talked about life, men, clothes and everyday "girls stuff." We never dwelt on the fact that she was ill. One of the things I admired so much about Mel was that she was an extremely positive person. I am not sure if it was because of her current situation but I realized that there was something different about Melissa. She became a better person. Her bright personality and her usual smile were a constant feature in our countless conversations. Melissa was a true gem and a jewel in my life. Words cannot sufficiently express how much she touched me as a person and also as a friend. I wish to this day that I was brave and strong as she was, as she battled this terrible illness.

A Tribute to my friend Melissa

I am plagued by the demon of guilt because during the time when her health was seriously deteriorating, she begged me on many occasions to visit her and to even spend a day with her. Unfortunately, this did not happen although we had many good telephone conversations. But I now realize that what she wanted most, above everything else, was my presence. She wanted me to be with her but I did not make the time for her. I truly regret not being there. Do not make the same mistake I did. Don't ever be too busy to spend time with the people that matter the most to you. I can't change the past but I can ensure that I don't make this mistake in the future. Melissa touched my life in a most sincere way. I'm so sorry Mel for not letting you know how much you really mattered to me.

Although I cannot go back and reclaim the lost moments that I should have spent with you, I want you to know you will always live on in the priceless memories we shared. Mel, you have left an indelible mark on my life and because of you I continue to seek to be the best friend I can be in my daily life. I no longer take my friendships for granted because time is precious and my friends are worth my time. I love you so much and I keep your picture right by my bedside, so that with every move I make you are there with me. It's as if a part of me secretly wants to spend time with you even; though you are not physically here. I don't want to let go of any part of you. Take care of yourself. See you in heaven mi chile!

P. S. As I had promised you, I wore full pink at your thanksgiving service, as I know that you did not want any dull colours. Keep sweet, love you to pieces.

Melissa and I at a one day
Retreat in January 2003

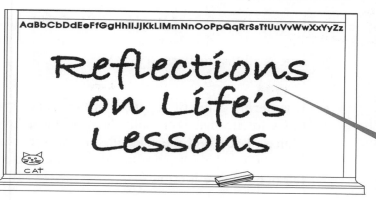

Melissa taught me many lessons. Here are some of them:

- It is my strong conviction that as long as you are born again through faith in Jesus Christ and have Him at the centre of your life, you are better able to cope with adversity. This was Melissa's experience. Consequently, she was able to use her illness to impact the life of others. As a result of my friendship with Melissa, I continue to believe that once you have God in your life, a divine peace is guaranteed.

- When you meet someone with AIDS please, please, please do not let the first question you ask be, *"How did you get infected?"* I know it may be tempting but do not give in to it. It is insensitive and in some ways, shows a lack of compassion. When I met Melissa I wanted to be her friend so that I could understand how she lived with the disease. If I were in her shoes, the last thing I would want is for someone to question me, upon introduction, about how I became infected. If you know someone who is infected with HIV/AIDS, I would encourage you to just be a friend. In due time, he or she will tell you what you desire to know. However, if they never do, that's okay. Just be there for them. Your presence and your love is all that matters.

- It is during some of the most difficult and trying times in life that you really feel the most loved. Melissa once told me that after being diagnosed with AIDS, she felt more loved than she had ever felt in her entire lifetime.

- Sometimes you have to take your eyes off yourself and help someone else. Being in a position to help others who are hurting is one of the true meanings of life. Thank you ever so much Melissa for teaching me this lesson.

- Melissa also reinforced something I have always believed, you can look like a diva even when you are feeling your worst. Sometimes looking like a diva is simply a state of mind.

Gone too Soon

On the day we met
I never knew you would be someone I would never forget
Our lives intersected at this moment in time
Because we both were experiencing traumas that caused
our lives to be on the line
We bonded immediately
because we both enjoyed laughter
And it was something we would do
from now and ever after
Little did I know that our moments together
would be short
As I still can't come to grips with it,
I've been continually distraught
With the thought that you are gone too soon.

I wish our meeting were under different circumstances
But as we all know,
life has a way of hurling us into tragedies
That will cause us to believe we are in a trance
However, focus on the little things
because it could be your last chance
As time progressed and we began to know
each other more
We drew strength from each other
so that we could endure
Because we had one thing in common,
we suffered in body as well as in soul

There were times when I thought that life was so unfair
As day by day I watched you sink in despair
But you fought hard and you fought strong
I had no idea that you wouldn't be here this long
As I still think you are gone too soon.

There were times when I felt like if the disease
were a person
I would grab it by the neck and choke its very life out
Because my mind was plagued with unanswered questions
and doubt
At the top of my lungs I wanted to scream and shout
Time and time again,
'Leave her alone you cruel disease!'
Would you be alive to fulfill your desires, your deeds?
She's too young, it's not her time yet,
I was not ready to say goodbye
How will I cope? How will I mourn?
I didn't know she would be gone this soon.

As I watched you impart your experience with this dreaded
disease to your audience
I felt so proud of you, you were brave, God,
you had courage!
You did it with care, class, compassion and fortitude…you
were fearless
You had your audience eating out of the palm
of your hands

I want you to know you touched so many lives
both rich and poor
You broke down walls of discrimination
and barriers of separation
And you did it in fine style,
you impacted my own life
Beyond imagination,
secretly I wished I were as brave as you.
I want you to know that you impacted so many lives
During your time here on earth
If you didn't know it I'm telling you
that you mattered
You didn't just pass through this life
Your living and dying made a difference
You mattered, my friend.

Words can't explain what it felt like to see you
in that casket
I hope it was a dream and life didn't seem
so surreal
I wished that any moment you would get up
and flash me your platinum smile
So that we could laugh again,
even if it was only for a while
You can't be gone! You can't be gone!
Please someone tell me it's not true!
There is so much we have not shared yet
Hello...goodbye
You are gone too soon

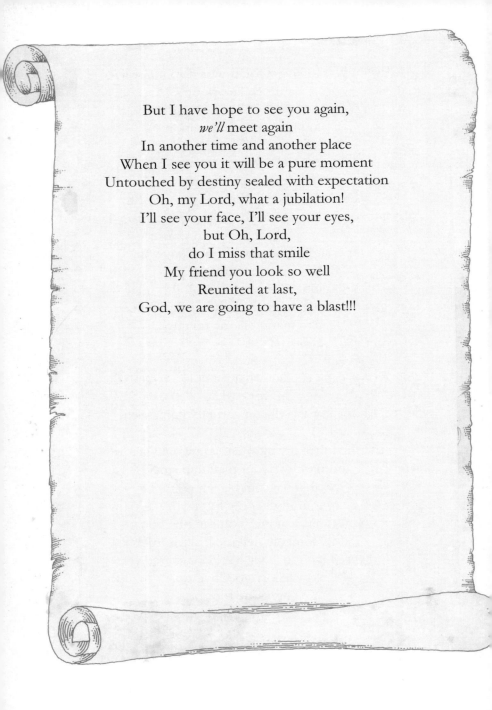

But I have hope to see you again,
we'll meet again
In another time and another place
When I see you it will be a pure moment
Untouched by destiny sealed with expectation
Oh, my Lord, what a jubilation!
I'll see your face, I'll see your eyes,
but Oh, Lord,
do I miss that smile
My friend you look so well
Reunited at last,
God, we are going to have a blast!!!

My
Unexpected
Journey

The Middle of Job

In the latter part of 2002, following three operations and faced with a situation with no solution in sight, I did what many Christians before me had done; I turned to the Book of Job in order to gain some understanding. I began an in-depth study of the book and the first fact that hit me was: Wow, did Brother Job have problems!

I recalled the many sermons I had heard based on the story of Job, but realized I had never heard one sermon drawn from the middle portion of the book. This was extended as well to quotations. There are some well-known and often quoted portions but very rarely did I hear something coming from the middle of the book. I will identify some of these portions.

This middle portion (chapters 6, 7, 10, 12 and 16-17) highlighted the fact that there were times when 'Brother Job' wanted to leave this life with all its troubles. There was frustration and anger; Job preferred death over life. He complained bitterly that his life had "no meaning." Job uttered some things to God that we would not dare say to Him. Yet, in the end, *"The LORD blessed the latter part of Job's life more than the first..."* (42:12-NIV).

I can identify with how Job felt because I have been at that place during my own valley experiences. I do not seek to ignore what is commonly considered Job's negative emotions, thoughts and expressions because they have helped me to fully appreciate that these things are all part of the journey. Job's story has a positive ending because God is the One who determines the beginning, the middle and the end.

Well-quoted Scriptures from the book of **Job** include:

"But he knows the way that I take; when he has tested me, I will come forth as gold."

(23:10- NIV)

"I will never admit you are in the right; till I die, I will not deny my integrity. I will maintain my righteousness and never let go of it; my conscience will not reproach me as long as I live."

(27:5-6-NIV)

"The Lord blessed the latter part of Job's life more than the first..."

(42:12-NIV)

My in-depth study yielded some gems that are *rarely quoted*. I offer three different versions of each in order to provide different perspectives:

6: 1-4

Then Job replied: **"If only my anguish could be weighed and all my misery be placed on the scales! It would surely outweigh the sand of the seas – no wonder my words have been impetuous. The arrows of the Almighty are in me, my spirit drinks in their poison; God's terrors are marshaled against me. "** (NIV)

Job said. *"It's impossible to weigh my misery and grief! They outweigh the sand along the beach, and that's why I have spoken without thinking first. The fearsome arrows of God All-Powerful have filled my soul with their poison."* (CEV)

Then Job answered, **"Oh, that my impatience and vexation might be [thoroughly] weighed and all my calamity be laid up over against them in the balances, one against the other [to see if my grief is unmanly]! For now it would be heavier than the sand of the sea; therefore my words have been rash and wild, [But it is] because the arrows of the Almighty are within me, the poison which my spirit drinks up; the terrors of God set themselves in array against me."** (AMP)

In the preceding verses Jobs says it is God's arrows that have poisoned his spirit. This seems to suggest that he blamed God for his adversity. Job was impatient and vexed; his words were *rash* and wild. In my own experience, I have hurled some *rash* and *wild* words at God. It is only by His mercy that I was not consumed.

7:13-16

"When I think my bed will comfort me and my couch will ease my complaint, even then you frighten me with dreams and terrify me with visions, so that I prefer strangling and death, rather than this body of mine. I despise my life; I would not live forever. Let me alone; my days have no meaning." (NIV)

" I go to bed, hoping for rest, but you torture me with terrible dreams. I'd rather choke to death than live in this body. Leave me alone and let me die; my life has no meaning."(CEV)

"When I say, My bed shall comfort me, my couch shall ease my complaint, Then You scare me with dreams and terrify me through visions, So that I would choose strangling, and death rather than these my bones. I loathe my life; I would not live forever: Let me alone, for my days are a breath (futility)." (AMP)

These verses reveal that it is neither strange nor unique to experience *"days of no meaning to life."*

10: 1 - Job complains to God:

"I loathe my life; therefore I will give free rein to my complaint and speak out in the bitterness of my soul." (NIV)

"I am sick of life! And from my deep despair I complain to you, my God." (CEV)

"I am weary of my life and loathe it! I will give free expression to my complaint; I will speak in the bitterness of my soul." (AMP)

Job's comment here is noteworthy: *"I will give free rein to my complaint."* Simply, let me vent my feelings of agony and frustration. Let me pour out my complaint.

As Job's situation dragged on he became the laughing stock of his friends. Instead of encouragement he received ridicule.

12:4

"I have become a laughingstock to my friends, though I called upon God and he answered – a mere laughingstock, though righteous and blameless!" (NIV)

"I have always lived right, and God answered my prayers; now friends make fun of me." (CEV)

"I am become one who is a laughingstock to his friend; I, one whom God answered when he called upon Him – a just, upright (blameless) man – laughed to scorn!" (AMP)

There was a time when my life was a reflection of this verse. I had just returned from a visit to the ENT clinic and I was talking with one of my friends on the findings. During the conversation I blurted out, *"In spite of what is happening, I still want my husband and three children."* She looked at me and had a good laugh. *"You still believe in that dream?"* she asked cynically.

I remember my internal dialogue was, *"I see that you don't really believe."* I purposed in my heart that she would be the first person on the guest list for the wedding and for the blessing of baby number one.

I still believe that the desires of my heart will be fulfilled. The Word promises in **Psalm 84:11-KJV, "...*no good thing will he withhold from them that walk uprightly.*"** I am hanging on to that verse with the very core of my being.

As Job's suffering continued his agony increased and it appeared to Him that God was punishing him without mercy. He felt like God had given him over to his enemies to be destroyed.

16:11 – 14

"God has turned me over to evil men and thrown me into the clutches of the wicked. All was well with me, but he shattered me; he seized me by the neck and crushed me. He has made me his target; his arches surround me. Without pity he pierces my kidneys and spills my gall on the ground. Again and again he bursts upon me; he rushes at me like a warrior." (NIV)

"And God is the one who handed me over to this merciless mob. Everything was going well, until God grabbed my neck and shook me to pieces. God set me up as the target for his arrows, and without showing mercy, he slashed my stomach open, spilling out my insides. God never stops attacking." (CEV)

"God has delivered me to the ungodly (to the evil one) and cast me (headlong) into the hands of the wicked (Satan's host). I was living at ease, but (Satan) crushed me and broke me apart; yes he seized me by the neck and

dashed me in pieces; then he set me up for his target. [Satan's] arrows whiz around me. He slashed open my vitals and does not spare; he pours out my gall on the ground. [Satan] stabs me, making breach after breach and attacking again and again; he runs at me like a giant and irresistible warrior." (AMP)

Sometimes we may feel like Job when we experience adversity but learn to recognize at all times who is our real enemy. It is not God, it is the devil. Beware that at times the length of the trial can really blur our vision. Pain has a way of narrowing our vision of who God really is.

Job felt despair and hopelessness at the thought that his plans and desires had been shattered:

17:11

"My days have passed, my plans are shattered, and so are the desires of my heart." (NIV)

"My life is drawing to an end; hope has disappeared." (CEV)

"My days are past, my purposes and plans are frustrated; even the thoughts (desires and possessions) of my heart [are broken off]." (AMP)

When I reviewed my many journal entries about this trying experience, there were times when I begged God to take me home because everything was just too overwhelming. However, I never contemplated taking my own life. Since he gave no indication of taking me I continued to trust Him. I know my times are in His hands.

Elloraine Lothian

The verses that we have examined from the middle chapters of Job are not very easy to read and seemed even harder to quote as they expressed the intense feelings of emotional torment. Although my illness pales in comparison to Job's trials, I can honestly say most of the emotions he felt, I have also experienced. In some ways, I feel as if I am related to him. There were times I referred to myself as 'Sister Jobinella.' The journal entries that follow may seem *rash* and *wild,* to borrow Job's words, but I was just being real with the emotions I felt at the time.

Journal entry

September 8, 2005

Words fail to adequately describe how my body feels. I'm so numb right now it isn't funny… God please, I am begging you. I am writing with tears in my eyes. You have to do something… God, my back feels like it is splitting into two. My neck feels like it is about to fall off. My head hurts so badly. My entire body aches. I cannot continue like this, please God! No, I can't pray right now, all I can say is "God please!!! God please!!! God please!!! I cannot go on, period. I just cannot go on. Please God, I cannot go on. God please take me home. This is just too much, God!!! I cannot live like this…"

Journal Entry
September 16, 2005

I have just been awakened by pains. God, I don't know if you are hearing me but I'm tired of crying out to you. It is not humanly possible to continue like this anymore. My body just cannot handle these pains anymore. Please God, take me home. I cannot do this anymore. I cannot!!! My neck is killing me.
God, do you even understand?

You promised me healing, how do you expect me to live like this? I can't live like this anymore. I really don't want to hear anymore crap. Yes!!! Yes, crap!!!

...I cannot live like this anymore. I can't God!!! I can't!!! This is too much for one soul to bear. I have been living with pain for such a long time, I cannot do this anymore, do You hear me!!!

...Let me go God. Please, no more pain. No more anything. No more broken dreams. No more... just total blackness and that for me is more heavenly than this abyss that I am in right now...

My Apologetic Entry
September 17, 2005

God, last night was bad or should I say yesterday morning. I am not sure if I am sorry for what I wrote because, God, I was being truthful about my feelings. I don't want to say I'm sorry and don't mean it. I think my tone was harsh and rude but the truth is I was venting what I felt at the time.

God, I must be allowed to blow up once in a while because, if not, I might just explode with all that is simmering on my inside. I do want to say i don't feel like venting this morning, I feel like your surrendered warrior...

The book of Job has been of great comfort to me throughout the years. It has taught me some valuable lessons one of which is that I must be honest before God no matter how *rash* and *wild* my feelings or thoughts. God is the only one that truly understands exactly how I feel. He knows what I will say even before the words are formed in my thoughts. I now know that one of the ways to achieve intimacy with God is to be honest with Him.

The Bible says in **John 8:32- KJV**, ***"And you shall know the truth, and the truth shall make you free."*** It really does set us free. When I confront the truth about my emotions and I honestly express it, there is a release and so because I have been educated by my experience whenever I hear of situations where someone is mad at God and is venting I just smile because I have been there; done that.

In the latter part of the year 2002, I read the book, **"Disappointment with God"** by Philip Yancey and it is still one of my favorite books. In this book, Yancey makes reference to a young man named Douglas, who he described as a modern day Job. In the words of Douglas, *"I have learned to see beyond the physical reality in this world to the spiritual reality. We tend to think, 'Life should be fair because God is fair.' But God is not life. And if I confuse God with the physical reality of life – by expecting constant good health, for example – then I set myself up for a crashing disappointment."* These words reinforced the important fact that in order to continue to enjoy my life I must accept that life may not be fair. However, I have the assurance that God has plans to take care of me, not to abandon me, plans to give me the future I hope for. **(Jeremiah 29:11–The Message).**

I have truly learned to live this life beyond the physical realities, accepting the fact that my life is more than this illness. I do not always expect life to be fair but I have found a balance between life and death. I love and appreciate life and all its God-given treasures but I am grateful that like the Apostle Paul, I can say what is most important is that I accomplish my purpose in spite of my adversity **[2ⁿᵈ Timothy 4:4-8-The Message]**.

In another of his books, **"Where is God when it Hurts?** Philip Yancey states, *"The book of Job should nail a coffin lid over the idea that every time we suffer it's because God is punishing us or trying to tell us something."* I appreciated those words so much when I read them because I remember time and time again my internal dialogue was, *'I must have done something wrong for this illness to come my way.'* This is borne out in my poem, *"Trust Me"* (see page 92) where I almost convinced myself of that lie because my limited mind could not comprehend all that was happening, especially with this prolonged illness.

AaBbCbDdEeFfGgHhIiJjKkLlMmNnOoPpQqRrSsTtUuVvWwXxYyZz

Reflections on Life's Lessons

CAT

- One of the most important lessons to be learned from the book of Job is that God wants us to be honest with him. If you are hurting or angry with Him, tell Him. Vent your true feelings to God. It will be cathartic. When you are venting, God is not looking down from heaven, gasping at your choice of words or covering His mouth in shock and disbelief. I think that when you vent, God is sitting there listening and just thinking to himself, *"Let me know when you are finished because I will still be here with you. I will still love you with an everlasting love."* Time will never erase this truth.

- It is important to develop a solid relationship with God that is not based on the physical realities of this life. When things begin to fall apart your relationship with God keeps you steadfast. Behind every crisis you experience in this life, God will always be constant and consistent in His love and compassion. There is absolutely no doubt in my mind that the main reason I have survived the past few years of this illness is that of my solid relationship with God. It supersedes the physical realities of my life.

141

Lamentations of Job

May it never be; the day that I was born
May it be erased from history, may it be gone
Why was I not like a still born child?
Receiving no life for even a little while
I weep, I cry
I yearn to die
But death does not come for me
Each day my life is filled with such misery
Oh, what I feared most has finally come
Calamity comes upon me and I cannot run

I spend my every waking moment in discomfort
and displeasure
The weight of my grief no one can measure
I'm confused, it's boggling my mind
A fault in me I cannot find
No boast do I make to be perfect
But what action could elicit this effect?
Show me Master how have I fallen? I do not know,
I beg I beseech, I implore thee
Why is thy hand so heavy upon me?

I say this without a second thought
The counsel of my friends succinctly comes to naught
It is of no value, it has not helped me in any way
It would have aided more had they nothing to say
I know they think to themselves

that they are doing a good deed
But who told them,
they could speak in God's stead
God and I are not in malice,
He can speak directly to me
If he needed a mediator it would not be those three
How unbelievable,
the counsel of three not amounting to one
I look for comfort from my friends and yet I find none

Job talks to God: Is there no justice;
how can these things be?
I'm oppressed by God and no fault in me I see
I've gone from patiently enquiring to
aggressively demanding
Your actions to me are beyond my understanding
I knew all along that justice didn't exist in the world below
But that it also abides not in heaven this I didn't know
Many a time I see evil prosper, live a long and lavish life
Goodness oppressed continually with all manner of
stress and strife

Why am I oppressed so severely, so long?
What act could I have committed,
what could I have done wrong?
I am confused;
your motives are beyond my comprehension
I cannot fathom what act would deem me worthy
of such oppression

The counsel of my friends only amplify my affliction
Whatever I have done my recompense
is more than my portion
You have viciously, maliciously, senselessly,
relentlessly attacked
But it's not righteous fury that you exact
For I know my hands and heart are clean
Such injustice I have never seen

Job pondered: I was honored, respected above
all other men, revered
Whatever I would speak all wanted to hear
All young men sought me for direction,
hungered for my guidance
They were parched ground, I was their sustenance
And now things have so horribly changed
So sadistically rearranged
I am no longer brimming with prosperity
My future is filled with such uncertainty

I have become so familiar with discomfort,
no stranger to pain
Each day torment and grief is all that I gain
My skin is discolored and from me it falls
I cry out to God and even now He doesn't answer my call
Really how does one benefit from doing good?
What blessing comes to one for doing what one should?
I have no hidden sins, I have not lied
Have not rejoiced when an enemy died

I clothed the naked, fed the hungry
No reason for God's hand to be so heavily upon me
My heart is in such turmoil, such chaos, such unrest
What cruelty! I'm punished for doing my best
For living without reproach, without sin
What kind of madness is this I'm in?
If I have sinned, if there be any blemish in my integrity
Let God continue to be cruel to me
Let my hand fall from the socket
Let God take my life, and do whatever with it

Oh, what joy when I think of days of old
Long before this barbarous persecution of my soul
When God and I were friends, I spoke to Him consistently
I saw the blessing of his favor continually
I have gone from a man of honor; no one could dispute
To a common commoner of ill repute

God talks to Job: Let my accuser step forward, be bold and
speak that I may hear
Job replies: I spoke hastily God…. My circumstance seemed
to be more than I could bear
God talks to Job: You let it get to your head….
You spoke badly of me
You thought your situation was unjust and I didn't see
Can you display my power….
my awesome ability of creation?
Do you think I don't have total power
over every situation?

Job's confesses to God: I not only think it,
I know it
Total supremacy belongs to you and you alone
I lie prostrate before you I humbly submit
No problem do I have to my King to admit
You are all powerful, Your plans no one can preclude
It is blatantly obvious that my inquisitions were rude
I hate myself for doubting; I repent with ashes and dust
for my crime against Thee
I am comforted now not just by what I hear of you
but by what I see
crave your forgiveness now more than how I wanted
your justice before
I'm sure now that whatever you allow
I can endure..............

And so: Because Job overcame these trials and tests
His latter days more than his former were blessed
God did more than just amazingly restore
He gave Job more than He ever had before
Job was comforted by his family and friends

My
Unexpected
Journey

Cries of the Heart

An Intimate Moment with my Lover and Lord

Lord, I want to be a worshipper
I want to be drunk with Your Spirit
I want to be drunk with Your presence
Take me to a next level
God, let me worship You all night long
With my whole heart I want to worship You
With my whole heart I want to please You
With my whole heart I need Your touch
I need You more than I need
my very next breath.

God, please silence the longings in my soul
Help me to reveal the real me

Lord, unveil me
Don't let me hide sections of my heart from You
Lord, forgive me for not trusting You as I should
Quiet the noise within my soul.

Let me long for You every second of the day
Lord, when I think about You
I want to smile in an intimate way
I want to think about You and
cry tears of gratitude
Tears of love just for You
Tears of gratitude to You
Thank You for saving me

Lord, I don't know what
I would do without You in my life
Where would I be without You?
God, anoint my hands to bring You glory
Anoint my feet to go where You want me to go
Anoint my lips so they will only speak
of the wonders of who You are
I am amazed when I think of You
You are all I need
You are all I will ever want
Nobody, and I mean nobody,
can satisfy my whole being like You.

I want to melt before You
I want to know You as my Lover
I need to hear You whisper sweet revelations to me
That will melt me in Your presence
I want to know what it is like to always have You
on my mind.

Without You life has no meaning
You are the reason I want to live
You are the very essence of my existence
Every thing is mundane without You.
Lord, when I talk about You
I want them to see You, Jesus, through my eyes
I want people to be attracted to Your image in me
And be ministered to by how much I love
and talk about You.

It means so much to me,
to know You will always be there for me
No matter what I go through in this life
You will hold me
Embrace me
Cradle me
Love me
Always wanting what is best for me.

You never have a bad thought towards me
No matter the countless times
I have disappointed
and brought shame to Your name
Yet, Your hands are always outstretched
Why do You love me so?
I can't comprehend.

Everyday of my life I want to praise You
God, I open my soul to You
God, I open my heart to You
God, I open my mind to You
God, I open my spirit to You
God take all of me.

God, use me up
Open my eyes to opportunities
to bring glory to Your name
Let my life be a ministry unto You
God, I am desperate for You
I am frustrated in my soul because I need You so much
I want to love You, please You
I need You so badly
My mind will not be at peace unless
I have Your nearness
I can't exist without You
Oh God, Oh God, Oh God,
Come to me, Hold me
Be intimate with me
Love me like no one else can
Your love means everything to me.

God, be my comfort zone
Be my hiding place
Be my solace
Be my warm embrace.
Touch me in places
No one has ever touched
Know me inside out
I don't want to be without You.

Let me be lost in You
Lost in worship because I see only You
when I close my eyes
God I' m not satisfied with just one touch of You
I need another touch
Jesus I don't want You to stop touching my life
I want to be right with You
So always move in my life Lord.

I hold loosely to the things of this world
Because they too will pass away
God, I miss my time with You
God, I want to be created in You all over again
Make me new Jesus
I want the fire of God to burn out the dross in me
God I desperately want to be pure before You

I hunger for holiness
Dwell in my temple Lord
Help me to keep my temple clean
So that You can enter at any time
Inhabit my life
Take all of me, Lord
All of me…all of me…

Reflections on Life's Lessons

AaBbCcDdEeFfGgHhIiJjKkLlMmNnOoPpQqRrSsTtUuVvWwXxYyZz

- It has been the common experience of many persons that their most intimate moments with God have been during the worst trials of their lives. This has also been my experience. I felt intimate with God in an unfamiliar yet beautiful way; I was falling in love with the Sovereign God all over again at a time when it seems my life did not make any sense. I hope this will be your experience too. Allow Him to cradle you in His everlasting arms.

- Let us look at an excerpt of the intimate **(Psalm 139:13-16-The Message)**

"Oh yes, you shaped me first inside, then out;
you formed me in my mother's womb.
I thank you, High God—you're breathtaking!
Body and soul, I am marvelously made!
I worship in adoration—what a creation!
You know me inside and out,
you know every bone in my body;
You know exactly how I was made, bit by bit,
how I was sculpted from nothing into something.

Like an open book, you watched me grow from
conception to birth;
all the stages of my life were spread out before you,
The days of my life all prepared
before I'd even lived one day."

My
Unexpected
Journey

Stages of Faith

As the years progressed, I gained a deeper revelation and understanding of faith and how I could survive a prolonged trial. In the process, I identified four stages that my faith endured:

1. Strong faith

2. Weakened but surviving faith

3. Waning faith

4. Loyalty faith

Recognizing and living through these stages helped me to understand that I will experience fluctuations in my level of faith. However, I am comforted by the fact that whatever God starts He finishes **(Philippians 1:6-KJV)**.

I allegorized the concept by using a glass of water.

Stage One – Strong Faith

This was the initial stage of my situation where my faith was strong. My glass was full. I was resolute that God would come through. I reassured myself, *"I will overcome this, Satan; you will not have the victory."* Most of my Bible reading was done at this time. The Word was my daily bread as I saturated my mind with 'Faith Scriptures.' I read Scriptures such as:

- *"And all things whatsoever ye shall ask in prayer, believing, ye shall receive."* (Matthew 21:22 – KJV)

- *"...The effectual fervent prayer of a righteous man availeth much."* (James 5:16 – KJV)

- *"... greater is he that is in you, than he that is in the world."* (1 John 4:4 - KJV)

Many persons earnestly prayed and were united in their belief for my breakthrough. Consequently, doubt was just a fleeting thought pushed aside by powerful prayers. Encouragement from friends and loved ones propelled me to be committed. With sustained faith I moved on to the next stage.

Stage Two – Weakened but Surviving faith

My glass was now at the halfway mark. At this stage, almost a year had passed with no positive change. My belief that all would be well staggered but I maintained that God would change my situation. I continued to read the Word but not as much as I did in the previous stage. Some of the Scriptures that kept me grounded at this time were:

- *"He [Abraham] staggered not at the promise of God through unbelief; but was strong in faith,*

160

giving glory to God;" [Emphasis added] (**Romans 4:20-KJV**)

- *"...and calleth those things which be not as though they were."* (**Romans 4:17-KJV**)

I forced myself to see through the eyes of faith that my healing was imminent even though that did not appear to be my reality. Questions assaulted my mind: *"But God, I have been praying for such a long time. How is it that nothing has changed? Don't I have enough faith?"* I tried to rationalize what was happening to me.

I was tempted to give up on my belief for a breakthrough. I felt as if I were not praying the right prayers. Time and time again, I became frustrated and was tempted to complain but I did not. I made the commitment to meditate on Scriptures like **Habakkuk 2:3-NLT**, *"...these things I plan won't happen right away. Slowly, steadily, surely, the time approaches when the vision will be fulfilled. If it seems slow, wait patiently, for it will surely take place. It will not be delayed."* I was encouraged to wait patiently because deliverance would surely come. Anointed songs, sermons, and words of encouragement were vital for my survival at this time. In spite of how my body felt, I simply could not forgo my conviction.

Stage Three – Waning Faith

My glass was at the quarter mark. Over a year had passed and thoughts of giving up continued to plague me. The devil wanted me to doubt God and lose faith and I now had to aggressively fight against the demons of complaint, frustration and depression.

I shed many tears. I felt like David when he cried out: *"...be not thou far from me, O Lord: O my strength, haste thee to help me."* **(Psalm 22:19–KJV)**. At times, it seemed my prayers went as far as the ceiling and ricocheted to me like the cry of the prophet Jeremiah *"And though I cry and shout, he shuts out my prayers."* **(Lamentations 3:8–NLT)**. I thank God for the persons who prayed for me consistently when I did not have the strength to pray for myself.

I began to doubt God's love for me and was tempted to get angry with Him; and sometimes I did. There were days I did not talk, feel or think. I existed. The temptation to give up was overwhelming but although my faith was waning I hung on. I developed a quietness and confidence in God which yielded strength. As Scripture states, *"...in quietness and in confidence shall be your strength..."* *(*Isaiah 30:15-KJV). When I was experiencing that quiet confidence I would call those days my *Quiet Confidence Days (QCD)*. Deep within my soul I whispered to God, *"I still believe your words that you will come through for me."*

Stage Four – Loyalty Faith

My glass was now almost empty. Two or more years had passed and my situation remained unchanged. I was consoled that all God needed to work in any situation was mustard seed faith. As Scripture states, *"...If you have faith as a grain of mustard seed, ye shall say unto this mountain, Remove hence to yonder place; and it shall remove, and nothing shall be impossible unto you."* **(Matthew 17:20–KJV)**

Stage four was the hardest. I now battle spiritual and emotional weariness. At this point, I did not know what to believe anymore. Time had taken its toll. Tears became the order of my day; like David, *"I'm on a diet*

of tears – tears for breakfast, tears for supper." (Psalm
42:3 - The Message).

I was reassured that tears are "a language that God
understands". The Scripture states in **Psalm 30:5-KJV,**
*"...weeping may endure for a night, but joy cometh in
the morning."* I may be crying now but my joy is on its
way.

At this stage, I was living off the Scriptures I held
dear to my heart, as I did not have the strength to read
them. I pasted Scripture verses on my bedroom wall to
allow me to directly see and mediate on them daily. Two
of my favorite Scriptures carried me through this
extremely difficult stage: *"...Calm down, and learn that
I am God..."* (Psalm 46:10-CEV), and *"The Lord will
perfect that which concerneth me..."* (Psalm 138:8–KJV).

The urge to give up was more dominant than in any
of the previous stages. It was the Holy Spirit that
strengthened me to remain steadfast. With His help I
developed, "Loyalty Faith." Faith that is immune to the
ide a of giving up. I reaffirmed in my spirit, *"Giving up
is not an option because I have fought too many em
otional and spiritual battles to quit."*

When I was at this stage, it was knowing that God
will come through for me that kept me going. There was
a peace – a deep settled peace that everything will soon
be resolved.

Some Scriptures that helped me in stage four are
quoted below. I have used two different versions of the
Bible to present a fresh perspective.

1 Corinthians 2:9

*"...What eye has not seen and ear has not heard and
has not entered into the heart of man, [all that] God has*

prepared (made and keeps ready) for those who love Him [who hold Him in affectionate reverence, promptly obeying Him and gratefully recognizing the benefits He has bestowed]."(AMP)

"...What God has planned for people who love him is more than eyes have seen or ears have heard. It has never even entered our minds!" (CEV)

I John 4:4

"...Because He who lives in you is greater (mightier) than he who is in the world." (AMP)

"...God's spirit is in you and is more powerful than the one that is in the world." (CEV)

Hebrews 10:23

"So let us seize and hold fast and retain without wavering the hope we cherish and confess and our acknowledgement of it, for He Who promised is reliable (sure) and faithful to His word." (AMP)

"We must hold tightly to the hope that we say is ours. After all, we can trust the one who made the agreement with us."(CEV)

Jeremiah 29:11

"For I know the thoughts and plans that I have for you, says the Lord, thoughts and plans for welfare and peace and not for evil, to give you hope in your final outcome." (AMP)

"I will bless you with a future filled with hope – a future of success, not of suffering." (CEV)

Summary of all Four Stages

Stages one and two were foundation stages for me, as most of my Bible readings were done during these stages. This was important as I needed it for stages three and four when I did not have the strength to read the Word. Encouragement from my church family, friends and loved ones was dominant at these stages. So, in these early stages the encouragement strengthened me to get me through the next two stages.

Stages three and four were the most challenging. There were days when I did not even utter a word of prayer. My prayer life was almost non-existent. But thanks be to God, the Holy Spirit reminded me that when I did not know what to pray, He the Holy Spirit, would pray for me. As Scripture reassured me, ***"And the Holy Spirit helps us in our distress. For we don't even know what we should pray for, nor how we should pray. But the Holy Spirit prays for us with groanings that cannot be expressed in words."*** **(Romans 8:26-NLT)**

It was also during these times that family, friends and other believers interceded for me. Often times I did not declare the Word of God as I should because the overwhelming nature of the situation had left me feeling powerless. However, the Holy Spirit sustained me through my faith journey and thanks to Him, I continue to hold on for my breakthrough whatever form it may take.

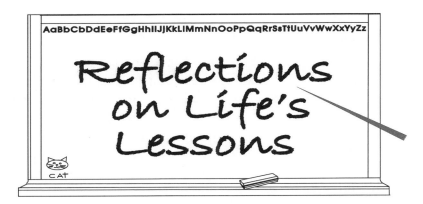

- There were several things to note as I went through each of the different stages of faith. For example, time diminished my faith. At times, we will indeed experience very low faith but the reality is we have to remain steadfast in our belief in God. We build our faith in God by reading the Word or meditating upon it, fasting and prayer and watering our souls with anointed songs (sometimes all that is needed to lift our faith is a song for the soul). I have learned these are *survival strategies;* they help us to hold on.

- It's okay when you can't pray deep prayers. Do not be discouraged when you can't even read your Bible. However, one thing you should always do, learn to meditate upon the Word. Paste Scriptures on the walls if you need to, so that, you see them on a daily basis. No matter what the situation, God is not going to miss His cue, to tell the devil his time is up and answer your prayer. Whatever you are going through it's just a season of your life because *it too will* pass. **1 Peter 5:10-NLT** states, **"...After you have suffered a little while, he will** *restore, support, and strengthen you, and he will place you on a firm foundation."* Friends, hold on for a little while longer.

- At every stage, the Word is our lifeline to fight against complaint, depression, frustration, doubt and weariness. It admonishes us, *"So then faith cometh by hearing, and hearing by the word of God."* **(Romans 10:17-KJV).** The Word is the key to strengthening our faith. We cannot make it without the Word.

- Seek to develop 'Loyalty Faith.' In your situation, refuse to give up even as time progresses and that situation does not change. Don't quit, you may do so just before your breakthrough comes.

167

Hold on

"Hold on! To What? How?
I want my breakthrough now
I've had enough
Never dreamed things would be this tough"
That was me at some point shouting
at my circumstances
Wondering what was happening;
was God doing this?
But I observed,
I learned that there were stages to faith
I saw again, that truly my God is great

No end to my trials, I could see
But composure resided somewhere in me
In the beginning my faith was strong
I trusted in God to carry me on
Then it seemed
Chaos like I've never dreamed
My breakthrough appeared to be late
I dug deeper, I tried to wait
Rescue looked futile;
I felt my Savior never came
Did God hear the petitions I made again
and again?

Perhaps it was circumstances to see if I
had what it takes
Yes, everything could have been a matter
of testing my faith
So I buckled down and held on,
even though doubt plagued me
I held on to scriptures that were dearest to me
But to be honest I could not reassure
Could not push myself to believe any more

Yet, a part of me refused to let go
Peace that surpasses understanding,
I came to know
The voices telling me to give up and reminding me
how long I've been praying
I realized one day I could no longer hear
what they were saying
I was committed, a determined warrior to the end
Loyalty extraordinaire to Christ my friend
I learned the final stage of faith,
the concept of surrender fled my mind

Nowhere in me, doubt could I find
I was tested, tried and I believe found to be true
Through my faith,
I endured all the devil tried to do

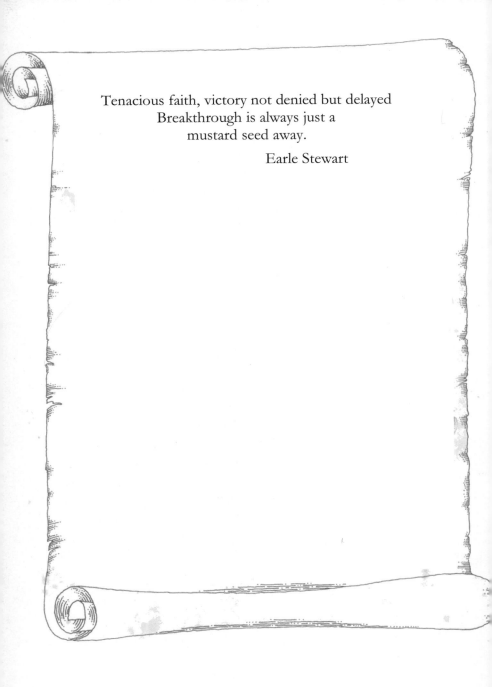

Tenacious faith, victory not denied but delayed
Breakthrough is always just a
mustard seed away.

Earle Stewart

My
Unexpected
Journey

Final Thoughts

As I write these final thoughts, I still have not done another surgery. The tumor now protrudes visibly from the left side of my neck and attracts more attention because of how big it has grown. Also, it has extended into my upper chest area and is displacing structures in that region. Subsequently, I suffer grave discomfort in my body. At this point, I am surviving purely by faith. As the Scripture says, *"For we walk by faith and not by sight"* (2nd Corinthians 5:7- KJV). Moreover, this *one thing* I know: No matter how many surgeries I may do, it will never diminish my love for God or my faith in Him.

I have surrendered the outcome of this illness to God. I am at a place of acceptance where I can honestly say that whatever God chooses to do, I trust Him. I trust His sovereignty; I may not understand it, but I trust Him. He is still hope, my solace, and the very reason for my existence. After all that I have endured, I still want God to rule and reign in my life. I can't imagine my life without Him.

I do not in any way believe that this is my final trial. I am sure that I will have more trials to encounter in the future but my consolation is that God is with me and that makes it alright. I may not understand how He works as **Isaiah 55:8 – 9 -KJV** declares,

"For my thoughts are not your thoughts, neither are your ways my ways, saith the Lord. For as the heavens are higher than the earth, so are my ways higher than your ways, and my thoughts than your thoughts."

We cannot always fathom God. If we could understand all His ways and thoughts, then He would not be God. However, I do know, as the songwriter so boldly states: *"God is too wise to be mistaken. He is too good to be unkind."*

I am just passing through this life. My last breath here will be my first in eternity. No wonder the Scripture says, *"If in this life only we have hope in Christ, we are of all men most miserable."*(1 Corinthians 15:19-*KJV*)

I have learned to develop a relationship with God that is not tied to the physical realities of this life. So, when the realities change my faith remains anchored. This is one of the reasons I am where I am today in the long battle with this illness.

In the book, **"Taught By Pain,"** four contributors wrote about their experiences with various kinds of pain and how they coped. One of these contributors, Barbara Piller, really put things in perspective when she said:

"One lesson I have learned in all this is that Christians cannot expect to have charmed lives…Being a Christian is not a sort of insurance policy. We must take the knocks as well, and as much, as anybody else. Christian happiness cannot be rooted in other people, in health or worldly fortunes. It must rest in the assurance that we have a Heavenly Father who will see that all things work together for good."

I encountered weary days as I passed through the different hardships on this journey. Those are days when I felt like I could not make it; but I held on by God's grace. I wrote the poem, "Days" for my friend, Wesley, when he was experiencing a trying time. He told me it put the situation in perspective for him. Here is what I said then:

Days

There are days when you feel
Like you can't go on
There are days, you just want to give in
To feelings of doubt, despondency,
melancholy, fear
Days when you can't fake it
Days when you can't take it
You sigh and wonder why is it worth a try?

Days when you are left stranded in pain
Thinking life is vain
Days when you don't want to move
You sit and allow the blanket of hopelessness
to consume you

But those days come and they go
That's the way it is
Be comforted that
Those days don't last
In time they'll be of the past.

In my own experience, there have been times when I was tempted to suppress my tears because it is felt that tears are an indication of weakness. However, I have discovered that God did not give me tear ducts for souvenirs and after I have cried, there is always a sense of peace that assures me everything is going to be alright. I have shed uncontrollable tears during my battle with this tumor. I have felt like 'Jeremena' (the sister of the weeping prophet Jeremiah) on countless occasions, giving free rein to weeping. I now know that crying is also a part of the journey.

I have learned that we have to be careful of the words we speak. That is why I do not allow myself to live in "Complaint City." If I complain, I have the wisdom to make it very short. If I have one negative thing to say I will quickly cancel it with a positive. For example, on a terrible pain day, I get a call from a friend enquiring how I was doing. My response was, *"The pain is driving me crazy but it could be worse."* If I do not have anything positive to say I will just simply keep silent. I am very mindful of the Word that says: ***"Death and life are in the power of the tongue: and they that love it shall eat the fruit thereof."*** (Proverbs 18:21 –KJV)

At times, our attitude in the fire (hardships or fiery trials) is important and the following story brings out that truth. The story is told of a woman who wanted to understand how **Malachi 3:3-TLB** *"Like a refiner of silver he will sit and closely watch as the dross is burned away...refining them...so that they will do their work for God with pure hearts* relates to our walk with God. So, she called and made an appointment with a silversmith.

Without mentioning anything beyond a general interest in the process, she sat and observed him work! She watched as he held the silver over the fire, explaining that in order to burn away every impurity, he had to keep it in the middle where it was hottest. She asked him if he usually sat in front of the fire for the entire time.

"Yes," he replied, "Not only do I have to hold it, I must watch it. If I leave it there even a moment too long it will be destroyed instead of being refined."

After thinking about that for a while she asked, "How do you know when the process is complete?" Smiling, the silversmith replied, "That's easy, I see my face reflected in it."

The point of this story is that God will only take you out of the fire when He sees His reflection in you.

After I read that story I remember asking God, *"Are you sure you haven't seen your reflection in me yet?"* Well, I am still in the situation...However, I am encouraged by the fact that I met Jesus in the fire He was there long before I stepped in. In the fire, I gained:

- New levels of intimacy with God. I wrote "Cries of the Heart" (see chapter 10) at a time when I cried out for intimacy with Him and The Awesome, Perfect Creator of the universe reached out to romance the soul of His imperfect daughter.

- New levels of revelation knowledge from the Word of God. In my own experience, one of the Scriptures that has become a foundation for all my petitions to God is **Matthew 24:35 - NIV.** It states, *"Heaven and earth will pass away but my words will never pass away."* This verse propelled me to prove God, time and time again throughout this difficult period and He has always come through.

- Insights into my destiny; that is, God's divine purpose for my life. I thought, since God had allowed me to endure a fiery trial it was not for me to rebel against the process as it may be His way of ushering me into His divine plan.

There are times when the Scriptures will be the only thing that get you through your trial. Invest in Bible commentaries and different versions of the Bible.

Know that God will indeed make up for your trying times. Remember *the hotter the battle the sweeter the victory*. Here are two verses to meditate on. They were of great comfort to me and still are:

(Joel 2:25-CEV), *"I, the Lord your God, will make up for the losses caused by those swarms and swarms of locusts I sent to attack."*

(2 Corinthians 4:16 – 17-The Message) *"So we're not giving up. How could we! Even though on the outside it often looks like things are falling apart on us, on the inside, where God is making new life, not a day goes by without his unfolding grace. These hard times are small potatoes compared to the coming good times, the lavish celebration prepared for us. There is far more here than meets the eye."*

The latter Scripture refers to hard times as *'small potatoes.'* It has reminded me that my experiences are only *'small potatoes'* compared to the good times that are ahead. There are lavish celebrations that God has prepared for me at the end of all my trials, tests and hardships.

There are times when the prolonged illness gets progressively worse and I wonder if God has amnesia and is deaf to my prayers. I may even begin to doubt His love. But I have learned not to believe the lies of the devil. God loves and cares for me. He even bottles my tears. **Psalm 56:8 - AMP** declares, *"You number and record my wanderings; put my tears into Your bottle…"*

God will never forget me. He has imprinted me on the palm of his hands. **Isaiah 49:16-AMP** states, *"Behold, I have indelibly imprinted (tattooed a picture of) you on the palm of each of My hands..."* Wow!!! That's awesome.

Learn to separate truth, facts, and feelings. Truth remains unchanged. It is timeless. The Word of God is our truth. What God said two thousand years ago was truth then and it is still the same today.

Facts are real. They can be proven in that there is always evidence, for example, X-rays prove that the tumor is growing in my neck and upper chest area. That is a medical fact. However, according to the Word of God; the truth that I stand on is in **Isaiah 53:5 – KJV** which states, *"But he was wounded for our transgressions, he was bruised for our iniquities: the chastisement of our peace was upon him; and with his stripes we are healed."* Based on that Scripture, I can claim my healing regardless of how my body looks or feels. My reality is based upon the truth, which is more powerful than any medical fact.

Feelings change and that is why I cannot allow my feelings to govern my life. That would be very detrimental. There are times when I become upset and angry and feel as if I could lay my hands upon someone and it was not to pray for them. If I gave into those feelings, there would be many persons with bruised bodies. Sometimes we have to encourage ourselves, *"Yes, this is what I am feeling but what is it that I know? I know truth... that governs my life."*

While I am going through my challenging experiences with this illness, I cannot allow the mental torment of it to take my spirit. It may have my body but I cannot give it my spirit. That's the reason I continue to push myself to go to the beach and enjoy the simple pleasures of nature. I fight for my spirit on a regular basis. On my worst pain days, I still try to look like a 'diva' in order to keep the essence of my spirit. So, I fight...fight... fight.

I know that there are situations where persons may be praying for divine physical healing for a loved one. The individual may be a quadriplegic in a wheelchair, suffering from multiple sclerosis or battling a rare type of cancer for a long time. You have prayed and believed with all your heart and hoped for a miracle but the person died. You may feel disappointed with God. You may be angry and feel justified with your anger. With my little knowledge on the subject of suffering I will not attempt to explain on God's behalf. Instead, let us examine my own situation.

If I pass on, not having received physical healing, I hope that I would have left a legacy that will inspire persons to really live regardless of whatever dreadful or heart-breaking situation they may encounter on this journey of life. I know, with God's help, I did fight this tumor and I won! My life became more meaningful because of it. My faith grew. I fell deeply in love with God all over again that at times I blushed when I talked about Him.

I truly lived a full life, not just existed; I know that I've gone to a better place where my body won't experience pain anymore. In his book, **"The Power of the Powerless,"** theologian Jürgen Moltmann points out, *"True health is the strength to live, the strength to suffer, and the strength to die. Health is not a condition of my body; it is the power of my soul to cope with the varying conditions of that body."*

Stand

What do you do when life has given you more sorrow
Than any mortal soul can bear?
And you get so overwhelmed that the last thing
you want to do is share?
What do you do when your tears have been your meat,
day and night?
When you no longer have the energy,
you no longer want to fight.
You stand, stand when all your dreams,
Goals and aspirations are in pieces at your feet.
And all your battles have ended in defeat
You feel like you can't go on
No desire, nothing compelling you to carry on.
What's the point to life any more?
Is anything worth it, is anything sure?
Though you can't comprehend,
You don't understand you *must* stand.

For those who walk uprightly,
He promised no good thing will he withhold
Master of all circumstances *He is* in control.
But often we wonder if this promise is true
For desolation is present in all we do.
So, in the midst of all your questions and doubts
And all you want to do is scream and shout

You stand, you stand in the uncertainty of it all
As time and time again your prayers
have hit the wall
No food on the table and your bank
account is low
Got paid already so there is no where else to go
You have stretched your last dollar to its limit
You want to throw up your hands
you want to quit
What do you do? You stand, you stand.

I know the temptation is there to compromise
Yes, Satan will present a Sugar Daddy
to fill you with lies
But don't back down, **stand,**
God sees and He knows
He is able to provide and in time it will show
The Lord has promised you your life partner.
Yes, Mr. or Mrs. Right
But he or she seems to be no where in sight
Your heart has been broken so many times
You wonder how it is still beating
So many around you find love through lies
and cheating.
But you stand even though it means you
stand alone
No one there to comfort you,
no one to call your own

Do not despair wrap your thoughts around the
Lover of your soul.

What do you do when life has given you
The one, two, three and your world collapse
right at your feet?
The marriage to the one you said would last
Is now a thing of the past
You stand, you believe, you trust
You trust God to come through for you
in *His* time
Even though if the truth be told
you are going out of your mind
So you stand, you stand on his promises
that cannot fail
Stand because Satan will not prevail.

So when all is said and you've done
all that you can do
You turn to the promises of God that are always
faithful and true.
You stand because God has promised that
He will perfect that which concerneth you
You stand because eyes has not seen not ears heard,
Nor has it entered into the heart of man
All that God has prepared for those who love Him
and still stand.

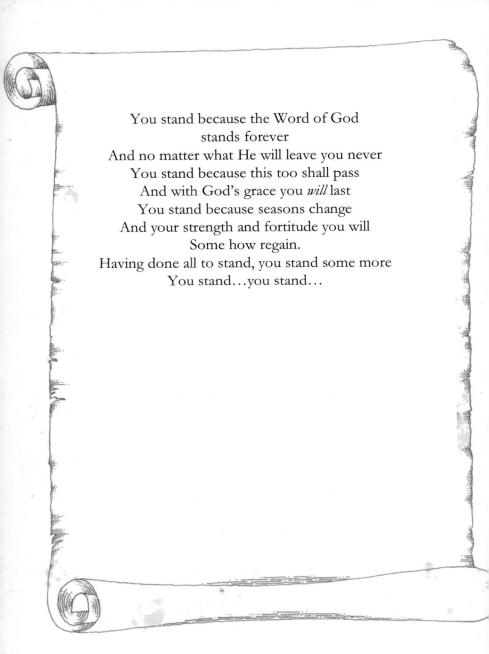

You stand because the Word of God
stands forever
And no matter what He will leave you never
You stand because this too shall pass
And with God's grace you *will* last
You stand because seasons change
And your strength and fortitude you will
Some how regain.
Having done all to stand, you stand some more
You stand…you stand…

My
Unexpected
Journey

Plea to the Unsaved

Thank you for taking the time to read this book. If you are not a Christian, it would not be complete without extending an invitation to you to accept Jesus Christ as your Savior and to make Him Lord of your life.

Let's have a heart-to-heart talk. God loves you unconditionally. You cannot do anything to make Him love you anymore or any less. He loves you just as you are. Yes, with all your faults and weaknesses and the many mistakes you have made and will make. Nobody can ever love you the way God loves you. A love that is inexplicable, incomprehensible and measureless.

I implore you; give Him a chance in your life. God will transform you into a new person. He will make you whole. Please, I am begging you to give Him a chance. Your life is empty without Him. You were created to have a relationship with Him.

187

You were born with a void that only He can fill. You may try to fill your life with sex, drugs and material things, but only God can truly fill that void. He gives you the best deal that life has to offer, that is, hope beyond this life.

May I share with you the fact that my relationship with God is the only thing that gives my life meaning. So, I am offering you this invitation to 'life.' Let God be Lord over your life, and experience a new existence with Him. Until you have experienced a relationship with Christ you will not realize how meaningful and fulfilling life can be; one that is filled with peace, purpose and prosperity. You can make this decision right now. Will you say this prayer with me?

Lord Jesus, I come to you acknowledging that I am a sinner. I believe that You died and rose from the dead for my sins and because of that my sins can be forgiven and I can be born again and receive new life. I am asking you to come into my life now, forgive me of all my sins, wash me and make me new. Please create in me a clean heart and renew a right spirit within me. I accept forgiveness and new life through You, My Redeemer and say, Thank you Lord. In Jesus name I pray Amen.

My friend:

If you prayed that prayer and meant it with all your heart, you are now a child of God, adopted into God's family and having the same rights as Jesus His Son. God's Word tells us: *"The Spirit itself beareth witness with our spirit, that we are the children of God: And if children, then heirs; heirs of God, and joint-heirs with Christ;..."* (Romans 8:16 -17- KJV).

Having made this momentous decision you will want to grow in the Lord. You will do that by reading His

Word, praying, telling others about Him and very importantly finding a place for fellowship where the Word is preached uncompromisingly. May God bless you as you grow and mature in Him.

Father

Thank You for the work you have done in these lives. I leave them in your loving care, in Jesus' Name. Amen.

The diagnosis of the condition is called Aggressive Fibromatosis, also known as Desmoid Tumors. These tumors are uncommon. The estimated incidence in the general population is 2-4 per million people per year. They do not have the capacity to spread distantly (metastasize) throughout the body as a result they are considered to be benign and not malignant. Even though benign they can cause destruction of vital structures (for example bones) or organs and in some cases may lead to death.

Causes of Fibromatosis

The etiology of Desmoid tumors is unknown. It may occur sporadically, or link to familial adenomatous polyposis (FAP) (a genetic abnormality). The linkage between Desmoid

191

Tumors and FAP has given some major clues about the genetic basis of at least some tumors. There have also been cases where they have been linked to scar tissues received as a result of surgical procedures. For example, there have been cases where Desmoid tumors have been seen in pregnant women who have done C-sections.

The Treatment of Fibromatosis

The treatment options for Desmoid tumors include:
1. Hormonal Therapy
2. Surgery
3. Radiation
4. Chemotherapy

Desmoid tumors can be persistent and complex in nature and no single treatment method will result in 100% remission. Whatever method of treatment that works for one person may or may not work for another and each option has it own risks. The most popular method of treating Desmoid tumors is usually surgical removal depending on its size and location when it is diagnosed. In some cases surgical removal is followed by radiation or chemotherapy. This is done in order to destroy any remaining tumor cells. However, it is to be noted that often times more than one treatment type is required. For example, surgery, radiation and chemotherapy may be necessary in treating one person for these tumors.

Vernon K Sondak. MD
H.Lee Moffitt Cancer and Research Institute
Tampa Florida

Official Scan Results for Medical Research

CT Scan of Neck & Chest results (February 14, 2002)

Pre and post contrast of the neck were done. There is a large soft tissue mass (6.5 x 4.9 x 10 cm) in the left side of the neck. It extends superiorly from the level of the cricoid cartilage to the level of the aortic arch inferiorly. The mass does not contain any calification and shows mild enhancement post IV contrast administration. There is associated compression of the left internal jugular vein and multiple collaterals are seen in the left side of the neck. There is erosion of the left anterior aspect of the

T1 vertebra and extension of the mass posterior to the trachea. The mass is in intimate contact with the left side of the esophagus and superiorly displaces it slightly to the right.

Impression: Pre Vertebral tumor/ R/o Neurogenic tumor

MRI Scan of Neck & Chest results
(April 17, 2002)

There is a large left paraspinal mass extending from the level of C6 down into the superior mediastinum where it abuts the aortic arch. It is 9.8 cm in cephalocaudal extent and 6.8 x 5.3 cm in cross section. There is erosion of the bodies of C6, C7 and T1 on the left side and encroachment on the left intervertebral foramina. The left vertebral artery is encased from its origin to the level of the left intervertebral foramina at C6. The left sided exiting nerve roots down to C6 appear normal. The exiting C7 nerve root is displaced by the mass. The exiting T1 nerve roots appears intimately related to the mass. The mass lies beneath the scalene muscles indents the lung apex and abuts the aortic arch and great vessels.

Impression: - Left paraspinal neurofibroma with compression of left vertebral artery, erosion of C6 – T1 and intimate contact with the left T1 nerve root.

CT scan of Neck and Chest results (June 2005)

3 mm and 5 mm axial tomograms were performed from the soft palate to the level of the pulmonary trunk before and after I.V. contrast. A large enhancing soft tissue is seen extending from the level of the carotid bifurcation inferiorly to the arch of the aorta. It lies posterior to the carotid artery, displacing the artery anteriorly, in the neck. The left lobe of the thyroid gland is also displaced anteriorly and the trachea, larynx and esophagus are displaced to the right. The mass appears to completely encase the left common cartiod artery as it enters the superior mediastinum. Within the mediastinum it extends to the left and posteriorly, partially encasing the left subclavian artery. The innominate veins, right innominate artery and left carotid artery lie anterior to the mass within the mediastinum. The mass measures a maximum diameter of 7 x 6.3 cm in the neck and 7.1 x 4.8 cm in the thorax. Surgical clips are noted. There is erosion of C7, T1 and T2 vertebrae.

Impression: - Large mass of fibromatosis intimately related to left common carotid artery and left subclavian artery.

Chapter1*: Mild What!!!*
Pathologic Basis of Diseases *,*
Robbins, Cotran, Kumar, 3rd Edition,
W. B. Saunders Publishing Company 1984 USA
(Pages 1432 – 1433)

Chapter 3: The Tumor was back!!!
Reprinted by permission. Tommy Barnett, Jill
Briscoe, Nancie Carmichael, Gordon MacDonald,
John C. Maxwell, J.I. Packer, Charles Stanley, John
Trent Shelia Walsh. ***Desert Experiences,*** Personal
Reflections on finding God's Presence and Promise in
Hard Times. Compilation Copyright © 2001 Thomas

Chapter 9: The Middle of Job
Philip Yancey, *Disappointment with God*
Three Questions No One Asks Aloud, Guidepost
Edition is published by Zondervan Publishing House
Copyright ©1988 Philip Yancey. (Page183)

Philip Yancey, *Where is God when it Hurts?*
American Red Cross Edition Copyright © 1990, 1977
by Philip Yancey. Zondervan Publishing House,
Grand Rapids Michigan. (Page 89)

Chapter 12: Final Thoughts
Mary Endersbee, *Taught By Pain, Falcon Books*
Published by the Church Pastoral Aid Society London
Copyright © Mary Endersbee 1970 (Page 74)

Word for Today, Caribbean Edition, Are you in the
refiner's fire? Issue 11 (Page 44)

Let me hear from you......

Thank you for sharing my journey through the pages of this book.

I would love to hear about your journey as well, please email me at ellorainelola@yahoo.com.

Also, you can visit myunexpectedjourney.com for more information about this book.